Thi[illegible] 3

PHONICS FOR READING

ANITA ARCHER
JAMES FLOOD
DIANE LAPP
LINDA LUNGREN

ILLUSTRATOR
LAUREL AIELLO

CURRICULUM ASSOCIATES®, Inc.

ISBN 0-89187-993-5

North Billerica, MA 01862

15 14 13 12 11 10 9 8 7 6

Table of Contents

LESSON 1

■ **New Sound.** Say the word.

moon

A. New Words. Say each sound. Say each word.

1.	food	soon	feed
2.	flirt	broom	flow
3.	spoon	brain	smooth
4.	choose	sport	tooth

5. Soon we shall be home.
6. I need to get a broom.
7. Jill likes to eat with her spoon.
8. It is hard to choose the winner.

B. Challenge Words. Say the words.

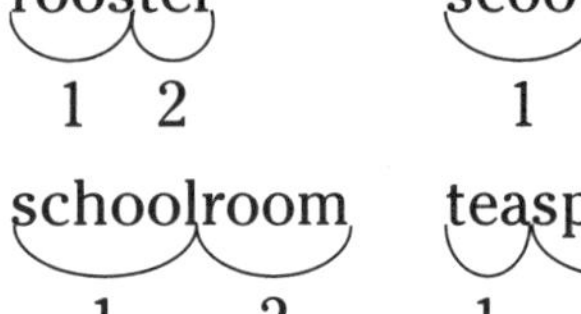
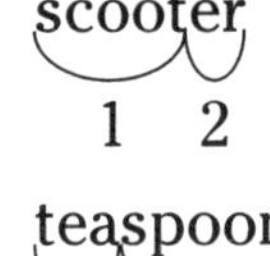
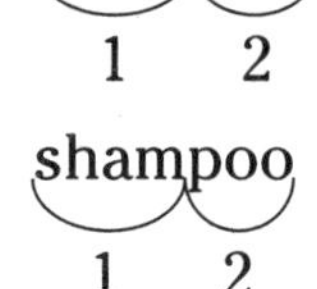

rooster 1 2	scooter 1 2	moonlight 1 2	cartoon 1 2	toothbrush 1 2
schoolroom 1 2	teaspoon 1 2	shampoo 1 2	raccoon 1 2	afternoon 1 2 3

C. Word Parts. Say the words.

unlock distrust agreeable handful

D. Words with Word Parts. Say the words.

1.	unreal	discard	dismay	unchain
2.	helpful	teachable	drinkable	faithful
3.	unthinkable	disgusting	distrustful	ungrateful

E. Sight Words. Say the words.

all	call	hall	ball	tall
because	through	also	about	
care	find	were	one	your
who	some	how	many	

F. Passages. Read each part of the story. Write the story part number under the picture that goes with each story part.

Tooth Care

Part 1

When you were born, you did not have teeth. The food you ate had to be soft
17 because you did not have teeth. You ate soft food with a spoon. After a while, one tooth
35 came through your gums. That may have hurt a bit. Soon after that, more and more
51 teeth came through your gums. A grown-up has thirty-two (32) teeth. Some are big and
66 some are not. They are all hard, white, and smooth.
76 Because your teeth are important to you, you must take care of them. You need your
92 teeth to eat your food. Teeth are also part of a big smile. It is not hard to take care of
113 your teeth; it just takes time.

Part 2

119 It is very important to keep your teeth clean. The food you eat can stick to your
136 teeth. If the food stays there, it will hurt the tooth. The best way to clean your teeth is
155 to brush them with a toothbrush. A toothbrush cleans your teeth as a broom cleans
170 the pavement. You should brush your teeth up and down to get all of the hidden food
187 bits. Brush your teeth when you get up in the morning and when you go to bed each
205 night. You should also brush your teeth after each meal. Brushing your teeth is the
220 best way for you to care for your teeth.

Part 3

229 A dentist helps you take care of your teeth. A dentist cleans your teeth and shows
245 you the best way to brush them. Your dentist tells you the best toothbrush to get.
261 Dentists also help if you have pain in your gums or teeth. The pain tells you to go see
280 your dentist. It may mean you are not taking care of your teeth right.
294 If food stays on a tooth, it can make a hole in the tooth. A hole in the tooth hurts.
314 Your dentist will find the hole and fill it. This will make the pain stop.
329 If you do not like pain, brush your teeth after each meal. You should see your dentist
346 for checkups, too. If you take care of your teeth, they will serve you well.
361

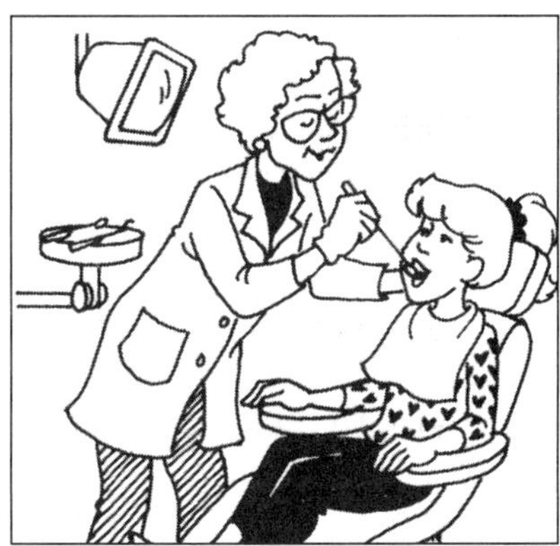

_______________ _______________ _______________

G. Practice Activity 1. Read each question. Look back at the story on page 5. Fill in each blank with the best word.

Part 1

1. **WHY** do we have to eat soft food when we are little?

   We have to eat soft food because we have no ____________________.

2. **HOW** many teeth do grown-ups have?

   Grown-ups have ____________________ teeth.

3. **WHY** are teeth important?

   Teeth help us eat ____________________.

Part 2

4. **WHAT** is the best way to clean your teeth?

   The best way to clean your teeth is to ____________________ them with a ____________________.

5. **WHEN** should you brush your teeth?

   You should brush your teeth when you get up in the morning and before you go to ____________________. You should also brush your teeth after each ____________________.

Part 3

6. **WHO** can clean your teeth and show you how to brush them?

   A ____________________ can clean your teeth and show you how to brush them.

7. **WHAT** might happen if food stays on a tooth?

   The food might make a ____________________ in the tooth.

8. **HOW** can you take care of your teeth?

   You can ____________________ your teeth and see your dentist for ____________________.

☐ Correct

H. Practice Activity 2. Underline all the endings that make sense.

1. A girl can ____________________.
   a. sit in a schoolroom
   b. stir tea with a teaspoon
   c. clean her teeth with a toothbrush
   d. shampoo a horse in a sink

2. Fred can ____________________.
   a. sweep moonlight with a broom
   b. ride a scooter to the store
   c. see moonlight during the afternoon
   d. feed peanuts to a cartoon

☐ Correct

I. Practice Activity 3. Fill in each blank with the best word.

handful	**unlock**	**drinkable**	**helpful**	**dismay**	**agreeable**
unreal	**discard**	**grateful**	**teachable**	**unchain**	**distrustful**

1. Please ____________________ the car so we can get in.
2. Janis fed a ____________________ of peanuts to the raccoon.
3. Tom fixed the broken lock and painted the gate. Tom was very ____________________.
4. The water was clean. It was ____________________.
5. The day was like a dream. It seemed ____________________ to Janis.
6. If you throw something away, you ____________________ it.
7. Barb was very ____________________ for the help we gave her.
8. If you can teach a dog a trick, the dog is ____________________.
9. You should be ____________________ of someone who steals.
10. Pete groaned with ____________________ as he missed the ball.
11. Joan would be more ____________________ if she would smile sometimes.
12. ____________________ the dog's leash from the gate, please.

☐ Correct

LESSON 2

A. **New Words.** Say each sound. Say each word.

1. moon cool show
2. noon sheet tool
3. shoot moose boast
4. boost moan snooze
5. Rover likes to bark at the moon.
6. What is the noon meeting about?
7. The moose roamed through the forest.
8. Dad will take a snooze before dinner.

B. **Challenge Words.** Say the words.

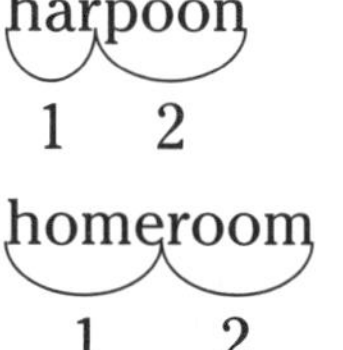
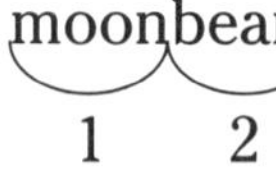
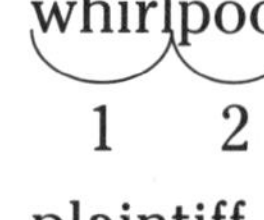
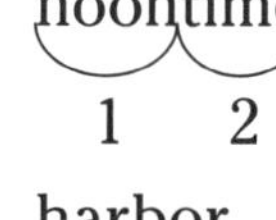

harpoon (1 2)	moonbeam (1 2)	whirlpool (1 2)	noontime (1 2)	monsoon (1 2)
homeroom (1 2)	classroom (1 2)	plaintiff (1 2)	harbor (1 2)	increase (1 2)

C. **Word Parts.** Say the words.

unlock distrust agreeable handful

D. **Words with Word Parts.** Say the words.

1. display unsnap unrest disturb
2. fixable painful reachable faithful
3. distasteful unmendable unsinkable unskillful

E. **Sight Words.** Say the words.

all	tall	ball	fall	call
because	also	through	about	find
where	your	now	how	why

F. Passages. Read each part of the story. Write the story part number under the picture that goes with each story part.

Chuck and His Teeth

Part 1

It was nine and time for Chuck to go to bed. He got into bed and felt the cool sheets. He lay in bed, but he could not sleep because the moon was too bright. He got up and shut the drapes. Then he got back into his bed and went to sleep.

"Rats!" Tom Tooth said to his sister. "I was hoping he got up to clean us. That beef he had for dinner is still stuck on my back."

"Part of this morning's bran muffin is right next to me, too," said Nan Tooth. "This is all very distasteful. I hate to say it, but it may be time for some pain. Chuck needs a boost."

Part 2

About noon the next day, Chuck sat down to eat lunch. He felt a bit of pain in his tooth, but the pain was not bad. Then he had a drink of milk. "My tooth hurts!" he said with a moan. "Mom! My tooth hurts a lot. Can you make it stop?"

"I can't make it stop hurting, Chuck. We will have to go to the dentist. She will check your teeth and make the pain stop. I will check with the nurse to see when we can go." Mom left the room and came back after three or four minutes. "The dentist can see you at three. For now, stay still and rest."

Part 3

"Well, Chuck, that tooth will be fine soon," said the dentist. "I can also see that you need to brush your teeth more. I will clean your teeth and show you how to take care of your teeth at home. Your toothbrush is an important tool, but you must use it more than you have been. Let me show you," she said as she started to clean Chuck's teeth.

"I feel so clean and fresh!" Nan Tooth said. "It's a shame we had to do it that way, Tom. I feel bad about it."

"Chuck is smart, Nan," said Tom Tooth. "I think he will brush us more now. He needs us as much as we need him. I bet we will have a clean and neat home from this day on!"

______________________ ______________________ ______________________

G. **Practice Activity 1.** Read each question. Look back at the story on page 9. Fill in each blank with the best word.

Part 1

1. **WHY** did Chuck get up?

   Chuck got up to shut the ________________.

2. **WHAT** did Tom Tooth hope that Chuck would do?

   Tom Tooth hoped that Chuck would ________________ his teeth.

3. **WHAT** did Nan Tooth say that Chuck needed?

   Nan Tooth said that it might be time for some ________________.

Part 2

4. **WHAT** did Chuck tell his mom?

   Chuck said, "My tooth ________________!"

5. **WHERE** did Chuck have to go?

   Chuck had to go to the ________________.

Part 3

6. **WHAT** did the dentist tell Chuck?

   The dentist said, "You need to ________________ your teeth more."

7. **WHAT** did the dentist do?

   The dentist ________________ Chuck's teeth.

8. **HOW** did Nan Tooth and Tom Tooth feel?

   They felt fresh and ________________.

☐ Correct

H. Practice Activity 2. Fill in each blank with the best word.

noontime	**toothbrush**	**classroom**	**scooter**
shampoo	**raccoon**	**moonlight**	**rooster**

1. Tom rode the __________________ down the road.
2. Dennis put the __________________ in the bathtub.
3. After lunch, the children went back to the __________________.
4. In the bright __________________, we could see the raccoons.
5. We saw the __________________ run inside the log.
6. The red __________________ wakes us up in the morning.
7. At the store, Janis got a green __________________ for her teeth.
8. Trish will wash the car at __________________.

☐ Correct

I. Practice Activity 3. Fill in each blank with the best word.

1. Janis will __________________ her jacket.
   unsnap unreal unchain
2. Barb and Fred are making a raft. Barb has a __________________ of nails.
   painful handful helpful
3. The lock broke, but I think it is __________________.
   fixable teachable drinkable
4. I don't like games. I __________________ them very much.
   discard dislike display
5. Dad is taking a nap. Do not __________________ him.
   disturb dislike distrust
6. The box is on the top shelf, but I think it is __________________.
   fixable teachable reachable

☐ Correct

LESSON 3

A. New Words. Say each sound. Say each word.

1.	room	loose	stool
2.	root	steal	roof
3.	booth	mood	beach
4.	hoop	lease	bloom

5. My little gray cat likes to sit on that stool.
6. Her tennis ball is stuck on the roof of your shed.
7. Ken's mood will be better after he gets some rest.
8. Who is the best person to enter the hoop contest?

B. Challenge Words. Say the words.

dustproof	booster	loosen	baboon	tattoo
foolproof	mushroom	drainpipe	president	innkeeper

C. Word Parts. Say the words.

unlock distrust agreeable handful

D. Words with Word Parts. Say the words.

1.	disown	unload	unleash	displease
2.	affordable	boastful	needful	harmful
3.	disagreeable	unfaithful	distressing	unhelpful

E. Sight Words. Say the words.

all	fall	call	hall	tall
about	because	want	through	also
put	now	one	find	been

F. **Passages.** Read each part of the story. Write the story part number under the picture that goes with each story part.

Room to Grow

Part 1

"No, Carl, you may not go until you clean your room. Look at it! I bet a baboon would
19 turn up his nose at it! I have been telling you for three days to clean it. If you start soon,
40 you could get to the beach by about noon." Then his mom left the room.
55 "This put me in a bad mood!" Carl said to his dog, Tattoo. "I want all of this stuff. There
75 is just too much for this room. Do you see that hoop? Coach Green gave it to me. I can't
95 part with it. I like that big stool, too. I got it cheap at a yard sale last week. I might use it
118 someday." Carl sat on the bed. "I need to think about this," he said to Tattoo.

Part 2

134 After a while, Carl got up. He started to pick things up. He made his bed. Then he slid
153 the hoop from Coach Green under the bed. "It fits, Tattoo," he said. "I wish the stool
170 were flat so I could slide it under the bed." Carl stopped and said, "My room is cleaner,
188 but I am still not through."
194 Carl dusted his desk and then swept with a broom. There was a lot of dust. Soon the
212 room started to look clean. "Well, Tattoo," Carl said, "what shall I do with that stool? It
229 may have been a steal, but it may have to go." Tattoo just gave Carl a glum look.
247 "Wait!" Carl yelled. "I have it!"

Part 3

253 Carl left his room and went down to the yard. When he came back, he had three pots
272 with plants in them. He put the stool in the corner by his window. He put one plant on
291 top of the stool and the rest on the steps.
301 "Mom," Carl yelled, "now my room is clean. Come and see it." Mom came in and
317 smiled. Carl's room was neat and clean. Then she saw the stool in the corner.
332 "It's more than a stool, Mom," Carl said. It is also a plant stand. Those plants need
349 light to grow. Look at this rose. It's about to bloom. I got the whole root when I dug it
369 up. Now may I go to the beach?"
377

__________ __________ __________

G. Practice Activity 1. Read each question. Look back at the story on page 13. Fill in each blank with the best word.

Part 1

1. **WHAT** did Carl have to do?

   Carl had to ________________ his room.

2. **WHO** gave Carl a hoop?

   ________________ ________________ gave Carl a hoop.

3. **WHERE** did Carl get the big stool?

   Carl got the stool at a ________________ ________________.

Part 2

4. **WHERE** did Carl put the hoop?

   Carl put the hoop under the ________________.

5. **WHAT** did Carl think he might have to get rid of?

   Carl felt he might have to get rid of the ________________.

Part 3

6. **WHAT** did Carl get from the yard?

   Carl got ________________ ________________ with plants in them.

7. **WHERE** did he put the plants?

   He put the plants on top of the stool and on its ________________.

8. **WHAT** was the stool now?

   The stool was a ________________ ________________.

☐ Correct

H. Practice Activity 2. Underline all the endings that make sense.

1. The children can __________ .
   a. ride on a moonbeam
   b. see a baboon at the zoo
   c. vote for a homeroom president
   d. shampoo a big baboon in the sink

2. After lunch, the art teacher will __________.
   a. go back to the classroom
   b. loosen the lids on the jars of paint
   c. sweep the moonlight into a box
   d. make a cartoon with a crayon

☐ Correct

I. Practice Activity 3. Fill in each blank with the best word.

1. Dad will ____________________ the fishing rods from the car.
   unchain unreal unload

2. Please do not ____________________ the children who are napping.
   displease disturb discard

3. Jeff ate a ____________________ of food.
   harmful spoonful helpful

4. Ann can fix the broken stool. The stool is ____________________.
   agreeable fixable teachable

5. Mr. Smith will ____________________ the classroom in the school.
   unsnap unrest unlock

6. Jane gave Bart a ____________________ of peanuts.
   skillful painful handful

7. Not all bugs are ____________________ to a garden.
   spoonful handful harmful

8. The cups on the top shelf are ____________________.
   teachable reachable agreeable

☐ Correct ☐ Checking up

LESSON 4

■ **New Sound.** Say the words.

saw fault

A. New Words. Say each sound. Say each word.

1.	yawn	fault	claw
2.	haul	float	draw
3.	spool	crawl	cool
4.	lawn	loan	cause

5. The cat's claw is sharp.
6. The truck will haul this load away.
7. They had to crawl through the cave.
8. Look at how green the lawn is!

B. Challenge Words. Say the words.

exhaust (1 2) author (1 2) auburn (1 2) August (1 2) drawing (1 2)

lawn mower (1 2 3) lawyer (1 2) igloo (1 2) imperfect (1 2 3) advertise (1 2 3)

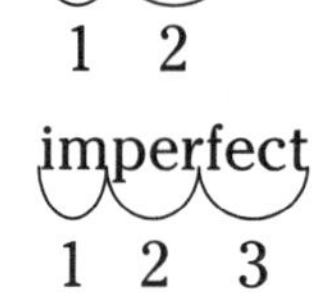

C. Word Parts. Say the words.

return preheat madness helpless

D. Words with Word Parts. Say the words.

1.	refill	unseen	prepay	discard
2.	endless	freshness	portable	grateful
3.	returnable	repayable	unthinkable	boastfulness
4.	unpreventable	distrustfulness		

E. Sight Words. Say the words.

other	another	mother	brother	
many	also	call	find	about
been	come	people	there	were

F. Passages. Read each part of the story. Write the story part number under the picture that goes with each story part.

Apollo 11 to the Moon

Part 1

People have been thinking about the moon for a long time. On a bright night, many
16 people look at the moon. Some people dream about the moon or make wishes on the
32 moon. Others see a man on the moon. Still others say the moon is made of cheese!
49 We get more and more facts about the moon each year. The moon has no light of its
67 own. The light we see comes from the sun, which is 400 times bigger than the moon.
84 There is also no wind on the moon.

Part 2

92 In 1969, three men went to the moon in a rocket called *Apollo 11. Apollo 11* needed help
110 to get to the moon. Some of the help came from a *Saturn* rocket. Its one job was to help
130 *Apollo 11* and the three men reach the moon. The *Saturn* rocket helped launch *Apollo 11.*
146 A big tractor called a "crawler" hauled *Apollo 11* and the *Saturn* rocket to the launch
162 pad. Soon they blasted off. After a short while, a part of the *Saturn* rocket came off.
179 That part of the *Saturn* rocket did not go to the moon with *Apollo 11.* This was the first
198 step in the plan to get *Apollo 11* to the moon. Then another part of the *Saturn* rocket
216 blasted off and sent *Apollo 11* speeding to the moon. *Apollo 11* had to get close to the
234 moon and into the moon's orbit.

Part 3

240 When the men got close to the moon, part of *Apollo 11* stayed in orbit. The other
257 part, with two men inside, landed on the moon. The men had many jobs to do, such as
275 finding some rocks to take home and taking many snapshots of the moon. When they
290 lifted off from the moon, they needed to lighten their load. They had to leave some
306 things on the moon, such as their backpacks and boots. Then they returned to the
321 other part of *Apollo 11* still in orbit.
329 *Apollo 11* left the moon's orbit and started the long trip home. The trip home was
345 much like the trip to the moon. All went well on the return trip, and *Apollo 11* splashed
363 down in the water as planned.
369 In 1969, three men went to the moon and returned. It was a trip they would not soon forget.
388

________ ________ ________

G. Practice Activity 1. Read each question. Look back at the story on page 17. Fill in each blank with the best word or number.

Part 1

1. **HOW** long have people been thinking about the moon?

   People have been thinking about the moon for a ____________________

   ____________________.

2. **WHERE** is the light coming from that we see on the moon?

   The light we see on the moon is coming from the ____________________.

3. **HOW** much bigger is the sun than the moon?

   The sun is ____________________ times bigger than the moon.

Part 2

4. **WHAT** did the *Saturn* rocket do?

   The *Saturn* rocket helped to ____________________ *Apollo 11*.

5. **WHAT** helped *Apollo 11* reach the launch pad?

   A big tractor called a "____________________" helped *Apollo 11* reach the launch pad.

Part 3

6. **WHAT** did the other part of *Apollo 11* do while one part landed on the moon?

   The other part of the *Apollo 11* craft stayed in ____________________.

7. **WHAT** did the men on the moon have to find?

   The men had to find ____________________.

8. **WHERE** did *Apollo 11* land on the return trip?

   Apollo 11 ____________________ down in the water on the return trip.

☐ Correct

H. **Practice Activity 2.** Fill in each blank with the best word.

August	**author**	**exhaust**	**president**
advertise	**classroom**	**lawyer**	**moonlight**

1. Mr. Martin will ____________________ the sale in this week's paper.
2. Some of the hottest days are in ____________________.
3. They voted for a ____________________ to run the club.
4. It was a dark night because there was very little ____________________.
5. After school, the teacher worked in his ____________________.
6. Black smoke came from the truck's ____________________ pipe.
7. Who is the ____________________ of this children's story?
8. He needs a ____________________ to help him win his rights.

☐ Correct

I. **Practice Activity 3.** Fill in each blank with the best word.

1. On Thursday, Fred will pay for the next three weeks of rent.
   Fred will ____________________ the rent.
   preheat / prevent / prepay
2. Jeff will fill the cups for the third time.
   Jeff will ____________________ the cups with coffee.
   return / refill / rerun
3. The buns were just baked.
   You will like the ____________________ of the buns.
   madness / coolness / freshness
4. Jill thanked us for helping her.
   She was very ____________________.
   grateful / spoonful / handful
5. The road went on and on.
   The road seemed ____________________.
   helpless / endless / nameless
6. You can take the TV from room to room.
   The TV is ____________________.
   portable / reachable / drinkable

☐ Correct

LESSON 5

A. New Words. Say each sound. Say each word.

1.	fraud	straw	stool
2.	dream	drawn	vault
3.	hawk	freed	shawl
4.	flow	flaw	flee

5. Our cow, Bessy, eats straw.
6. Is the vault made out of steel or copper?
7. Lin gave her mother a red silk shawl.
8. The painter corrected a flaw in his work.

B. Challenge Words. Say the words.

applause (1 2) coleslaw (1 2) withdrawn (1 2) sawdust (1 2) drawback (1 2)

autumn (1 2) sweepstakes (1 2) wayside (1 2) bridegroom (1 2) entertainment (1 2 3 4)

C. Word Parts. Say the words.

return preheat madness helpless

D. Words with Word Parts. Say the words.

1.	pretend	report	dismay	unhurt
2.	nameless	likeness	affordable	pocketful
3.	remarkable	distinctness	unteachable	unthankfulness

E. Sight Words. Say the words.

other	another	brother	mother	
many	also	animals	because	want
there	what	were	now	call

F. Passages. Read each part of the story. Write the story part number under the picture that goes with each story part.

The Art Show

Part 1

"What a way to spend the afternoon!" Paul said to his brother Fred. "I want to go to
18 the beach, but I have to go to the art show in the park. My art teacher said that we all
39 have to go to this show. Next week each of us has to report to the class. It's part of the
60 grade for the class," Paul moaned. "At least you said you would go with me, Fred. That
77 will make it less painful. Let's get our bikes and go now."
89 "Be a good sport, Paul," said Fred. "Many of the kids from your class will be at the art
108 show. It may turn into a fun afternoon. OK, let's go."

Part 2

119 Paul and Fred rode down the street to the park. When they got to the lawn on the
137 east side of the park, they saw hundreds of people. Some were selling things but many
153 others were just looking. Paul and Fred put the bikes in a bike rack and locked them.
170 Then they went to see what the artists had drawn.
180 "Look at this!" Paul said. "It's just a straw stuck to the side of a box. Is this art? It has
201 a name, too. It's called "Straw Dream." You can own it for $45. Who would pay $45 for
219 this? I hope this work of art is not a fraud. Let's go to the other end of this row."
239 On the way, they stopped to look at a portrait of a man with a hawk on his hand. "He
259 looks sad," Fred said. "He also looks like he is speaking to that hawk. Do you think the
277 hawk's claws are hurting the man?" he asked.

Part 3

285 Soon they came to a booth where a man on a stool was drawing portraits in ink. Paul
303 and Fred stopped to look. The artist worked very fast, and his drawings were flawless.
318 "What a remarkable likeness for such fast work!" Paul said in surprise. "Some of this art
334 is art after all!"
338 "There is a band playing on the lawn," Fred said. "We can go there for some
354 entertainment if you like."
358 "Who needs a band for entertainment?" Paul said with a grin. "When I saw Jill, she said
375 we had to go see a painting down this way. She said the painting is called "Artist's Flaw."
393 It's just a big white blank with a black border. I could do art like that! Let's go see it."
413

______________ ______________ ______________

G. Practice Activity 1. Read each question. Look back at the story on page 21. Fill in each blank with the best word or number.

Part 1

1. **WHERE** did Paul have to go?

   He had to go to an __________________ __________________ in the park.

2. **WHY** did Paul have to go?

   Paul had to go to the art show because his __________________

   __________________ said that his class had to go.

3. **WHO** said that he would go to the art show with Paul?

   Paul's brother __________________ said that he would go to the art show with Paul.

Part 2

4. **WHAT** were people doing at the art show?

   Some people were __________________ things, but many others were just

   __________________.

5. **HOW** much did "Straw Dream" cost?

   "Straw Dream" cost __________________.

6. **WHAT** did the man in the portrait have on his hand?

   He had a __________________ on his hand.

Part 3

7. **WHAT** was the man in the booth doing?

   The man was __________________ portraits in ink.

8. **WHAT** painting did Paul and Fred go to see?

   Paul and Fred went to see a painting called "__________________

   __________________."

☐ Correct

H. Practice Activity 2. Fill in each blank with the best word.

coleslaw	**sweepstakes**	**bridegroom**	**applause**
entertainment	**autumn**	**drainpipe**	**sawdust**

1. Next to the lumber mill were piles of ________________.
2. The bride and the ________________ left after the wedding.
3. There was much ________________ when the play ended.
4. We ate ________________ at the picnic.
5. The ring fell down the sink's ________________.
6. The season after summer is ________________.
7. Do you think you could ever win the ________________?
8. For your ________________, I would like to sing a song.

☐ Correct

I. Practice Activity 3. Fill in each blank with the best word.

1. Mom will heat up the food left from last night's dinner.
   Mom will ________________ the food.
   reheat
   report
   return

2. The drawing looks just like Janis.
   The drawing is a perfect ________________ of Janis.
   freshness
   madness
   likeness

3. The doctor helps keep people well.
   The doctor hopes to ________________ illness.
   preheat
   pretend
   prevent

4. If you cannot get into a room, you may need to ________________ the door.
   unhurt
   unlock
   unseen

5. The work at the store never seemed to stop.
   The work seemed ________________.
   nameless
   helpless
   endless

6. Mr. Martin will take the TV back to the store.
   He will ________________ the TV to the store.
   refill
   return
   reheat

☐ Correct

LESSON 6

A. New Words. Say each sound. Say each word.

1.	law	choose	pause
2.	lawn	thaw	sprawl
3.	sprain	jaw	jar
4.	paw	throw	launch

5. Jane plans to study law next fall.
6. I hope the food does not thaw on the way to the picnic!
7. Did you see the size of that gorilla's jaw?
8. Will they launch this rocket at noon or at three o'clock?

B. Challenge Words. Say the words.

pauper 1 2	sawmill 1 2	because 1 2	seesaw 1 2	awesome 1 2
launder 1 2	autoharp 1 2 3	automatic 1 2 3 4	misinterpret 1 2 3 4	understood 1 2 3

C. Word Parts. Say the words.

return preheat madness helpless

D. Words with Word Parts. Say the words.

1.	rechoose	predict	unpack	disgust
2.	speechless	smoothness	bucketful	doable
3.	recorder	preventable	presentable	refillable

E. Sight Words. Say the words.

other	another	mother	brother	
many	through	also	one	want
about	would	how	from	now

F. Passages. Read each part of the story. Write the story part number under the picture that goes with each story part.

A Painful Lesson

Part 1

"We all miss you at school," Jan said to Trish. "I hope you got the card we sent.
18 Miss Parks let me choose the card because I said I would see you today." Trish smiled
35 but did not speak.
39 "This seems very odd," Jan said. "This is the first time I have seen you speechless.
55 Is your jaw still painful?" Jan stopped and then said in disgust, "I keep doing that! You
72 can't speak with that hurt jaw, yet I keep asking you about things! Let's play cards for
89 a while. Tell me when you need to take a rest."
100 They played a card game. After a while, Jan left and said she would be back soon.

Part 2

117 "Did you see Trish this afternoon?" Jan's mother asked when Jan got home. "I
131 understand she will have to rest for a long time."
141 "Yes, I saw her," Jan said. "We played cards for a while, but I left because she
158 seemed to be in pain. She has a broken jaw and three cracked ribs. Her left arm is also
177 sprained. That car crash caused a mess for Trish. She will miss a lot of school, too.
194 Miss Parks is taping some of the school lessons. Trish can play the tapes on her tape
211 recorder, but it's not the same as being in school with the rest of us. It must be hard
230 staying in bed all day," Jan said with a sigh.

Part 3

240 "It's a shame," Jan's mother said. "It's also too bad because her pain could have been
256 prevented. Trish's mother said Trish did not have her seat belt on. Think about it. Seat
272 belts can save lives. In fact, many people think we should have a seat belt law. I hope
290 you and your pals will not soon forget this lesson."
300

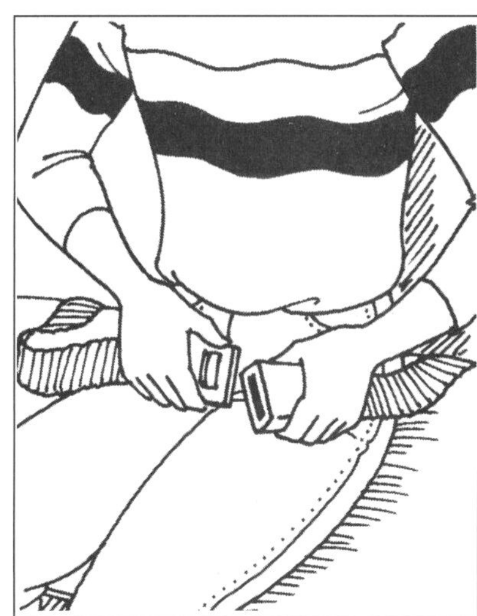

G. Practice Activity 1. Read each question. Look back at the story on page 25. Fill in each blank with the best word.

Part 1

1. **WHY** didn't Trish speak?

   Trish didn't speak because she hurt her ________________.

2. **WHO** came to see Trish?

   ________________ came to see Trish.

3. **WHAT** did Trish and Jan do?

   They played ________________.

Part 2

4. **HOW** did Trish get hurt?

   Trish was in a ________________ ________________.

5. **WHAT** must Trish do?

   Trish must stay in ________________ all day.

6. **HOW** is Miss Parks helping Trish?

   Miss Parks is ________________ some of the school lessons.

Part 3

7. **WHY** did Trish get hurt?

   Trish did not have her ________________ ________________ on.

8. **WHAT** can seat belts do?

   Seat belts can save ________________.

☐ Correct

H. Practice Activity 2. Fill in each blank with the best word.

straw	**yawn**	**haul**	**launch**
hawk	**drawn**	**fault**	**pause**

1. They hope to ________________ the rocket on Thursday afternoon.
2. Janis drank the smooth milk with a ________________.
3. Dennis will ________________ the junk away in his jeep.
4. Jim's car ran off the highway during the storm. It was not Jim's ________________.
5. Peg has ________________ three portraits in art class.
6. When Ted woke up from his nap, I saw him ________________.
7. I saw a big bird perched on the roof. I think the bird was a ________________.
8. There will be a short ________________, and then we will start the second part of the play.

☐ Correct

I. Practice Activity 3. Fill in each blank with the best word.

1. If you take things out of a box, you ________________ the box. — untie / unpack / unleash
2. If you cannot speak, you are ________________. — nameless / speechless / endless
3. If you tell people about something, you make a ________________. — refill / repay / report
4. If something can hurt you, it is ________________. — harmful / boastful / handful
5. If you can take something from room to room, it is ________________. — fixable / preventable / portable
6. If a painting looks like you, it is a good ________________. — freshness / madness / likeness

☐ Correct ☐ Checking Up

LESSON 7

■ **New Sound.** Say the words.

oil joy

A. New Words. Say each sound. Say each word.

1.	boil	boy	point
2.	paint	Roy	pawn
3.	joy	soil	goose
4.	coin	cool	noise

5. Turn the heat higher if you want to boil the broth.
6. Roy is the name of my horse.
7. The rose will grow better in potting soil.
8. This car makes a lot of noise.

B. Challenge Words. Say the words.

turmoil (1 2)	employ (1 2)	enjoy (1 2)	destroy (1 2)	tinfoil (1 2)
boycott (1 2)	joyride (1 2)	oyster (1 2)	appointment (1 2 3)	sharpshooter (1 2 3)

C. Word Parts. Say the words.

become delay fraction

D. Words with Word Parts. Say the words.

1.	beside	defrost	present	rethink
2.	action	mention	coolness	toothless
3.	belonging	detention	devotion	reflection

E. Sight Words. Say the words.

old	cold	told	gold	sold
one	other	many	another	about
want	all	there	come	what

F. Passages. Read each part of the story. Write the story part number under the picture that goes with each story part.

Roy's Coolness

Part 1

"I am sick of this! Day after day we sit in this room for no good reason. I want to play
21 and have fun. That's not too much to ask for, is it, Will?" said Sweet Thing.
37 "Hush, hush, Sweet Thing," Will said. "If you make too much noise, Roy will wake up.
53 That would destroy it for all of us. Besides, we still have each other. Let's enjoy what we
71 can and not mention what we can't fix. There, there, don't cry," said the old sharpshooter.
87 "I feel the same way," Bess said. "For a long time, I sat right next to Roy's bed. Now I
107 am with you in the dark, like a discarded dishrag. What's the point of this?" Bess said
124 with a sniff. With that, the toys all went to sleep.

Part 2

135 The boy named Roy woke up at six the next day. He put on his shirt and jeans and
154 dashed from the room.
158 "What could be *that* important?" asked Bess. "It's just six. He treats us as if we are just
176 toys, and I am not a toy! I am a bank with lots of bright coins in me. If he has no interest in
200 his other toys, these coins of mine could get him a *good* toy to play with," said Bess.
218 "What do you mean by a 'good' toy?" yelled Sweet Thing. "I am a paint-by-number kit,
236 and I have many good drawings left!"
243 "That's right," said the pawn from the chess set. "We are all good toys and games.
259 There must be another reason for Roy not to play with us."

Part 3

271 "Come, come," said the old sharpshooter. "This will not help us at all. Roy may have
287 an appointment to keep."
291 "I can't help it," said Sweet Thing. "Bess makes me boiling mad! Roy kept that bank
307 by his bed for a long time. Just because of that, she thinks she is better than the rest of
327 us." For a while, no toy spoke. Then Sweet Thing said, "Besides, Roy may have had one
344 appointment today, but that can't explain his actions these past three weeks. I think he
359 is boycotting us. What can he be doing with his time?" she asked with a sigh.
375

_______________ _______________ _______________

G. Practice Activity 1. Read each question. Look back at the story on page 29. Fill in each blank with the best word.

Part 1

1. **WHERE** were the toys?

   The toys were in a ________________.

2. **WHAT** did Sweet Thing want to do?

   She wanted to ________________ and have ________________.

3. **WHO** owned the toys?

   The toys belonged to ________________.

Part 2

4. **WHAT** did Roy do in the morning?

   Roy put on his ________________ and ________________ and dashed from the room.

5. **WHAT** was Bess?

   Bess was a ________________.

6. **WHAT** was Sweet Thing?

   Sweet Thing was a ________________-by-________________ kit.

Part 3

7. **HOW** long had Roy not played with his toys?

   Roy had not played with his toys for ________________ ________________.

8. **WHAT** did Sweet Thing think Roy was doing to the toys?

   Sweet Thing thought that Roy was ________________ the ________________.

☐ Correct

H. Practice Activity 2. Read the story. Fill in each blank with the best word.

On Mom's birthday, Roy said, "I am going to bake a cake for Mom. I will just follow the directions on the box. I hope Mom enjoys her birthday cake."

DIRECTIONS

1. Boil a cup of water.
2. Put the cake mix into a bowl.
3. Stir the boiling water into the cake mix.
4. Spoon the mix into a pan.

1. Roy wanted to make a ________________ cake for Mom.
   birthday direction spoon
2. First, Roy had to ________________ a cup of water.
   soil stir boil
3. Then he had to put the cake mix into a ________________.
   boil bowl pan
4. Next, he had to ________________ the water into the cake mix.
   boil spoon stir
5. Roy put the cake into the stove to ________________.
   rake make bake
6. Roy said, "I hope Mom will ________________ her birthday cake."
   paint cool enjoy

☐ Correct

I. Practice Activity 3. Fill in each blank with the better word.

1. Mark did not ________________ that he would be late. He did say that he had work to finish. — fraction / mention
2. The storm will ________________ the train. The train will be very late. — defrost / delay
3. The breeze at the beach was very cool. Because of the ________________, I put on a jacket. — toothless / coolness
4. Tom could not tell us much. He was ________________. — speechless / smoothness
5. You can take the TV to the basement. The TV is ________________. — likeable / portable
6. I can see my ________________ in the pool. — reflection / detention

☐ Correct

LESSON 8

A. New Words. Say each sound. Say each word.

1.	join	jail	toy
2.	tea	spoil	toil
3.	maul	Floyd	spool
4.	moist	crawl	Troy

5. It's fun to join a club during the summer.
6. The hot sun may spoil the ripe bananas.
7. Will Floyd drive to Florida next week?
8. The rag must be moist for it to clean the spill.

B. Challenge Words. Say the words.

soybean (1 2)	noiseless (1 2)	annoy (1 2)	loiter (1 2)	exploit (1 2)
toy shop (1 2)	charcoal (1 2)	corduroy (1 2 3)	employee (1 2 3)	employer (1 2 3)

C. Word Parts. Say the words.

become delay fraction

D. Words with Word Parts. Say the words.

1.	before	depart	prefer	remake
2.	section	lateness	lightness	portion
3.	re define	destruction	description	prevention

E. Sight Words. Say the words.

old	fold	cold	told	hold
give	other	about	through	find
all	would	were	there	want

F. Passages. Read each part of the story. Write the story part number under the picture that goes with each story part.

Annoyed Toys

Part 1

The days seemed to crawl by, and still Roy showed no interest in his toys. There was
17 a lot of gloom on the toy shelf. At times, Sweet Thing and Bess would fight, but the rest
36 of the time, there was no noise at all. Roy came to his room to sleep, but that was all.
56 Floyd the Moose made an effort to teach the game of chess to Troy the Puppet, but it
74 was no use. The pawn in the chess set liked to tease Troy. When Troy paused to think
92 about his next play, the pawn would jump to a different spot.
104 These were long, long days for the sad toys.

Part 2

113 "I cannot take too much more of this," Bess said on a Thursday afternoon. "Roy is
129 just spoiled. There's no other description that fits. Just because he has other things to
144 do, he keeps us here like we were in jail. I would prefer that he give us to some other
164 boy. We might give some joy to a different boy. Besides, I like to be needed, and I am
183 sick of all this fighting. That's the way I feel about it."
195 "Well, what are we going to do about it?" asked Sweet Thing. "I agree with you. I am
213 sick of all this fighting, too." The rest of the toys looked shocked. The old sharpshooter
229 smiled a sad smile.

Part 3

233 The next day was much like the other days. Floyd the Moose and Troy the Puppet
249 gave up trying to play chess. For a while they played a card game called Go Fish. "Give
267 me all your fives," said Troy.
273 "What a feat!" yelled Floyd. "Did you sneak a peek? I'm through! You have all my cards!"
290 Just then they saw Roy. The toys became noiseless. Roy went over to the shelf and
306 said to the toys, "I am very glad to see you all. Today was my last day in the school play. I
328 joined the play because it seemed like it would be fun, but I had to spend a lot of time at
349 school. I have missed playing with you." Roy stopped and then smiled as he reached for a
366 toy. He said, "Because the play is over, I can spend more time with all of you!"
383

______

______

______

G. **Practice Activity 1.** Read each question. Look back at the story on page 33. Fill in each blank with the best word.

Part 1

1. **WHY** was there gloom on the toy shelf?

   There was gloom on the toy shelf because Roy showed ________________ ________________ in his toys.

2. **WHAT** did Floyd try to do?

   He made an effort to teach the game of ________________ to Troy.

3. **WHAT** did the pawn do during the chess game?

   The pawn would jump to a different ________________.

Part 2

4. **WHAT** did Bess say about Roy?

   Bess said that Roy was ________________.

5. **WHAT** did Bess want Roy to do?

   Bess wanted Roy to give the toys to some other ________________.

Part 3

6. **WHAT** card game did Floyd and Troy play?

   They played ________________ ________________.

7. **WHY** had Roy not played with his toys?

   Roy had not played with his toys because he had joined a ________________ ________________.

8. **WHAT** will Roy do with his toys?

   Roy will spend more ________________ with his toys.

☐ Correct

H. Practice Activity 2. Read the story. Fill in the blank with the best word or words.

On Beth's third birthday, her sister made a big, moist birthday cake for her. Her mom and dad gave her toys, a green shirt, and corduroy pants. Beth liked being spoiled on her birthday. After she ate birthday cake, Beth went to the backyard to play. With a big spoon, Beth dug a road in the garden for her cars and trucks.

1. It was Beth's __________________ birthday.
   first third fifth
2. Beth's sister made her a ______________________________.
   green shirt moist cake big toy
3. Her mom and dad gave her __________________ pants.
   corduroy green yellow
4. Beth liked being __________________ on her birthday
   crawled joined spoiled
5. Beth went to play in the __________________.
   bedroom basement backyard
6. With a spoon, Beth dug a __________________ for her cars and trucks.
   boy road soil

Correct

I. Practice Activity 3. Fill in each blank with the better word.

1. Jeff plans to be a fisherman. Jeff will __________________ a fisherman. — before / become
2. The storm will make the train late. The storm will __________________ the train. — delay / defrost
3. The test had three parts. It had three __________________. — sections / mentions
4. The dress is too big for Jan. She will need to __________________ the dress. — remake / rebake
5. The train will leave at six. It will __________________ at six. — defrost / depart
6. The cake was very fresh. I liked the cake's __________________. — lateness / freshness
7. The stool was next to the desk. It was __________________ the desk. — beside / become
8. Doctors and nurses help us keep well. They like to __________________ illness. — pretend / prevent

Correct

LESSON 9

A. New Words. Say each sound. Say each word.

1.	coil	coat	coy
2.	toy	paints	points
3.	fail	foil	pawn
4.	toil	tool	poise

5. Grease the coil so it will not rust.
6. The speaker gave us some important points to remember.
7. Should he put the chicken on a sheet of foil?
8. You will gain poise as you grow older.

B. Challenge Words. Say the words.

enjoy 1 2	ointment 1 2	poison 1 2	convoy 1 2	broiler 1 2
avoid 1 2	embroider 1 2 3	disappoint 1 2 3	destroyer 1 2 3	enjoyment 1 2 3

C. Word Parts. Say the words.

become delay fraction

D. Words with Word Parts. Say the words.

1.	decay	belong	resold	redo
2.	traction	witness	suction	sleepless
3.	deduction	bemoaning	reaction	unmentionable

E. Sight Words. Say the words.

old	cold	sold	fold	told
give	many	other	also	through
come	were	there	work	find

F. Passages. Read each part of the story. Write the story part number under the picture that goes with each story part.

Toys

Part 1

Where do toys come from? Many would say that toys come from toy stores or other
16 big stores. Today many toys do come from stores. In the past, toys were made at home
33 or by people called toymakers.
38 Toys made in the past were carved and painted by hand. Many toys today are made
54 of plastic. They are different from past toys. They also may not last as long. In the past,
72 people saved toys that they liked and passed them on to other children to play with.

Part 2

88 A toymaker must enjoy working with his or hands. Toymakers must cut, saw, or carve
103 each part of the toy by hand. They must also make all the parts fit. If the parts do not
123 fit, the toymakers will have to redo some of them.
133 Tools like a saw or a drill can be helpful, but a toymaker's hands are the best tools.
151 When a toy is all made, the toymaker may sand it to make it smooth and then paint it.
170 The work takes time but gives joy to the toymaker. Toymakers think it is time well
186 spent because they can give such joy to children.

Part 3

195 Making toys for children to play with and enjoy is an art and a craft. Many people
212 who make toys sell them at arts and crafts shows. Most things at an arts and crafts
229 show are made by hand.
234 People like toys that have been made with devotion. Toys made by hand may cost a bit
251 more, but people understand that toymakers spent a lot of time and toil making them.
266 The next time you go to an arts and crafts show, look for a toymaker's booth. You
283 may find toys that were made by hand, like a boat to float in a tub.
299

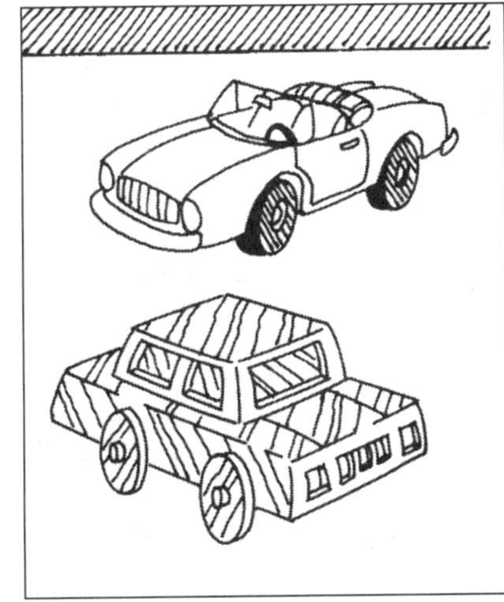

______ ______ ______

G. Practice Activity 1. Read each question. Look back at the story on page 37. Fill in each blank with the best word.

Part 1

1. **WHO** made toys in the past?

   In the past, __________________ made toys.

2. **WHAT** are many toys made of today?

   Today many toys are made of __________________.

3. **WHAT** did people do with toys in the past, since the toys lasted longer?

   People saved the toys and passed them on to other __________________.

Part 2

4. **WHAT** are a toymaker's best tools?

   A toymaker's __________________ are the best tools.

5. **HOW** might toymakers finish a toy?

   They might __________________ it to make it smooth and then

   __________________ it.

6. **WHY** do toymakers enjoy making toys?

   They enjoy making toys because the toys give such __________________

   to children.

Part 3

7. **WHERE** can you find handmade toys today?

   You can find handmade toys at an __________________ and

   __________________ show.

8. **WHY** do people like handmade toys?

   People like handmade toys because the toys are made with __________________.

☐ Correct

H. Practice Activity 2. Underline the endings that make sense.

1. On a hot afternoon, Carl might ________.
   a. enjoy a trip to the beach
   b. see a raccoon in the moonlight
   c. cut the lawn with his lawn mower
   d. stay in the shade to avoid a sunburn

2. On a dark night, Janis might ________.
   a. sit inside and embroider a pillowcase
   b. get a suntan at the beach
   c. enjoy an oyster dinner
   d. play her autoharp and sing

☐ Correct

I. Practice Activity 3. Fill in each blank with the best word.

sleepless	**before**	**destroy**	**redo**	**prefer**	**handful**
likeness	**decay**	**sections**	**belong**	**mention**	**readable**

1. Did you tell Jan that slacks are on sale? Did you ________________ that corduroy slacks are on sale?
2. I like hot dogs better than hamburgers. I ________________ hot dogs.
3. The box had five parts. It had five ________________.
4. The report had lots of mistakes. Janis had to ________________ the report.
5. These toys are Beth's. The toys ________________ to Beth.
6. The drawing looks very much like Pam. It is a close ________________.
7. I did not sleep last night. It was a ________________ night.
8. First we will make coleslaw. Then we will make hamburgers. We will make the coleslaw ________________ we make the hamburgers.
9. My handwriting is so messy. It is not very ________________.
10. If you do not clean your teeth, they will ________________.
11. My little sister gathered a ________________ of small shells.
12. An untended fire can ________________ a forest.

☐ Correct ☐ Checking Up

LESSON 10

■ **New Sound.** Say the word.

new

A. New Words. Say each sound. Say each word.

1. new noise grew
2. grain chew stew
3. news fee dew
4. drawn drew flew
5. Is that a new hair band?
6. I like stew made of beef, green beans, and corn.
7. The dew on the leaves of the tree was shining.
8. The bird flew to its nest in the beech tree.

B. Challenge Words. Say the words.

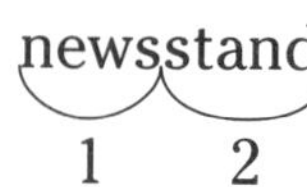

jewel (1 2)	newsstand (1 2)	newscast (1 2)	chewable (1 2)	New York (1 2)
newspaper (1 2 3)	screwdriver (1 2 3)	newsletter (1 2 3)	subscribe (1 2)	storekeeper (1 2 3)

C. Word Parts. Say the words.

inspect expand badly windy

D. Words with Word Parts. Say the words.

1. infect inflate demand export
2. nightly lucky likely reasonable
3. inspection exactly explainable infection

E. Sight Words. Say the words.

find mind kind

over give told about another

what who could come now good

F. Passages. Read each part of the story. Write the story part number under the picture that goes with each story part.

School Reporters

Part 1

Kris liked Miss Sanchez's class. But today he could not wait for the class to end.
16 At the end of class, Miss Sanchez was going to say who would work on the school
33 newspaper. Kris and some of the others had been waiting all week for this news.
48 At last Miss Sanchez said, "Boys and girls, I have some good news and some bad news.
65 The good news is that nine of you asked me about being on the newspaper staff. The bad
83 news is that we need just three more people. It was too hard for me to choose just three of
103 you. I have come up with a plan that I hope you will all like. Let me tell you about it."

Part 2

124 After class, Kris and some others sat down on the school's steps to chat about Miss
140 Sanchez's plan. "What a drag!" Kris said to Beth and Liz. "Who needs another paper to
156 do? Miss Sanchez has seen what we can do. She could have drawn names from a hat if
174 she had too many people to choose from." Kris groaned. "Another paper is all I need!"
190 "Be reasonable, Kris," Liz said. "If you stop to think about it, it's the best way to
207 show that you are the best person to work on the newspaper. Keep in mind that if
224 Miss Sanchez just drew names, being chosen to work on the newspaper would be
238 *luck*, not *skill*. Besides, your name may not have been drawn."
249 "That's right, Kris. We have a week to find a topic for a paper. It will have to be good,
269 so let's start thinking about *that*."

Part 3

275 During the week, Kris, Beth, and Liz met many times at Kris's home to discuss the
291 newspaper reports that they had to turn in soon. Kris had yet to start. "I can't help it," Kris
310 said. "This is a slow news week. I need to find exactly the right thing to do my paper on. It
331 has to have a new and different approach. It will come to me. Wait and see," he said.
349 "Do not wait too long, Kris," Beth said. "We have to turn these papers in next Thursday.
366 Besides, Miss Sanchez said that a good news reporter *finds* news. You can't just wait for it
383 to come to you. I have to go home. Good luck."
394

______ ______ ______

G. Practice Activity 1. Read each question. Look back at the story on page 41. Fill in each blank with the best word.

Part 1

1. Why did Kris want class to end?

   Kris wanted class to end because Miss Sanchez was going to say who could join the ________________ ________________.

2. Why didn't Miss Sanchez say who would be working on the newspaper staff?

   Miss Sanchez said it was too hard to ________________ just three people.

Part 2

3. What did Miss Sanchez ask the boys and girls to do next?

   Miss Sanchez asked them to write another ________________.

4. How did Kris want Miss Sanchez to choose the new staff members?

   Kris wanted Miss Sanchez to draw ________________ from a hat.

5. What did Kris need to do in the next week?

   Kris had to find a ________________ for his paper.

Part 3

6. What reason did Kris give for not picking a topic?

   Kris said that it was a ________________ ________________ week.

7. What kind of approach did Kris want his paper to have?

   Kris wanted his paper to have a ________________ and ________________ approach.

8. What did Miss Sanchez say about a good news reporter?

   Miss Sanchez said that a good news reporter ________________ news.

☐ Correct

H. Practice Activity 2. Fill in each blank with the better word or words.

1.	The ________________ will pay her ________________ this Thursday.	employees storekeeper
2.	The employer will ________________ in the ________________.	newspaper advertise
3.	Do you ________________ to a ________________?	newspaper subscribe
4.	Where is the ________________ story about the ________________ pills?	newspaper chewable
5.	The ________________ put the ________________ in the display case.	jewels storekeeper
6.	Jane got a ________________ from the ________________ chest.	screwdriver tool
7.	In the morning, I picked up a ________________ at the ________________.	newsstand newspaper
8.	Last summer, I went ________________ in ________________.	sightseeing New York

☐ Correct

I. Practice Activity 3. Fill in each blank with the best word.

nightly	**badly**	**demand**	**lucky**
inspect	**expert**	**windy**	**expand**

1. If the wind blows, it is ________________.
2. If you have lots of luck, you are ________________.
3. If you look at something with care, you ________________ it.
4. If you are very, very good at something, you are an ________________ at it.
5. If you ask for something that you want, you might ________________ it.
6. If something happens each night, it happens ________________.
7. If you did a bad job on a task, you did it ________________.
8. If a balloon got bigger and bigger, it would ________________.

☐ Correct

LESSON 11

A. New Words. Say each sound. Say each word.

1.	chew	paw	threw
2.	crew	join	blew
3.	grew	brew	shown
4.	joy	crawl	shrew

5. Chew your food well when you eat.
6. The wind blew the rain through the screen door.
7. The storekeeper will brew a pot of tea for the staff meeting.
8. In my garden, I saw a shrew, three green bugs, and one crow.

B. Challenge Words. Say the words.

sewer (1 2)	cashew (1 2)	unscrew (1 2)	mildew (1 2)	newborn (1 2)
newsreel (1 2)	crewneck (1 2)	seaplane (1 2)	jeweler (1 2 3)	authorize (1 2 3)

C. Word Parts. Say the words.

inspect expand badly windy

D. Words with Word Parts. Say the words.

1.	bemoan	intend	depend	exclaim
2.	noisy	sandy	brightly	slowly
3.	invention	delightful	expertly	prescription

E. Sight Words. Say the words.

find	mind	kind	
give	over	mother	one
told	your	about	
where	many	why	

F. Passages. Read each part of the story. Write the story part number under the picture that goes with each story part.

A Nose for News

Part 1

During the week, Kris spent a lot of time with pen and paper in hand. One by one he
19 threw the papers into the trash can. "Chewing your pen like that will not help, Kris," his
36 mother said one night. "There's not much time left," she said as she turned the TV on.
53 "Let's see what is on the nightly news. You might find that helpful." The TV news team
70 reported on a big brush fire, a new car invention, and a seaplane that had crashed not
87 far from the local beach.
92 "That's it!" Kris exclaimed. He started to grin. "I should have turned the TV on yesterday,"
108 he said. "Thanks, Mom. I can depend on you when I need to unscrew my brain!"

Part 2

124 On Thursday, Kris joined Liz and Beth on the steps of the school. They each had a
141 paper to turn in to Miss Sanchez. "It's about time," Liz said to Kris. "I see you have your
160 paper. What's it about?" she asked brightly.
167 "You will have to wait and see," Kris said. "I admit that's a rotten thing to say, but I
186 intend to keep still about it," he said with a grin. "Miss Sanchez said she would read
203 them all in class. You will have to wait until then."
214 Liz and Beth looked at each other and smiled. "OK, Kris," Liz said. "Have it your way.
231 We will all wait until Miss Sanchez reads them. Let's go—class is about to start."

Part 3

247 "Well, boys and girls, the time has come to read these papers. After I read them all
264 to you, I will ask you to vote for the top three. That will help me pick the new school
284 reporters. As I read, remember the important points that each report should mention:
298 who, what, where, when, and why." Then Miss Sanchez started to read the papers.
312 Beth's paper was all about the food served at school. The paper Liz turned in was
328 about the school play. Another paper was about the new fire station down the street.
343 One paper was on the art show in the park.
353 At last, Miss Sanchez got to Kris's paper. It was all about the seaplane crash. The
369 crew of the boat that had towed the plane to shore had given Kris the facts. When Miss
387 Sanchez finished Kris's story, everyone clapped and smiled at Kris. After the class had
401 voted, Kris was one of the new reporters.
409

____

____

____

G. Practice Activity 1. Read each question. Look back at the story on page 45. Fill in each blank with the best word.

Part 1

1. Where did Kris throw his many papers while trying to begin his story?

   He threw many papers into the ________________ ________________.

2. What did Kris's mother tell him to look at?

   She told him to look at the ________________ ________________ on TV.

Part 2

3. Where did Kris meet Liz and Beth?

   He met them on the ________________ of the ________________.

4. What did the children have?

   They each had a ________________ to turn in to Miss Sanchez.

Part 3

5. What important points did the papers need to mention?

   The papers had to tell ________________, ________________,

   ________________, ________________, and ________________.

6. What was Beth's paper about?

   Beth's paper was about the ________________ served at ________________.

7. What was Kris's paper about?

   His paper was about the ________________ ________________.

8. Who gave Kris the facts for his paper?

   The ________________ of the ________________ that had towed the plane to shore had given Kris the facts for his paper.

☐ Correct

H. Practice Activity 2. Fill in each blank with the better word.

1.	The __________________ locked the __________________ in the display case.	jeweler jewels
2.	The __________________ left his __________________ baby with his babysitter.	newborn gardener
3.	I asked the __________________ for a __________________ and a hammer.	storekeeper screwdriver
4.	Barb gets lots of __________________ from reading the __________________.	enjoyment newspaper
5.	The first __________________was about a __________________ pipe that broke during the night.	sewer newscast
6.	After dinner we had a __________________ nut pie and __________________.	cashew coffee
7.	The bad grade on the __________________ will __________________ Troy.	disappoint assignment
8.	Floyd __________________ his ride on the __________________.	enjoyed seaplane

☐ Correct

I. Practice Activity 3. Fill in each blank with the best word.

intend delightful depend sandy noisy invention brightly slowly

1. If you go to the beach, you are likely to get __________________.
2. If there is lots of noise in a room, the room is __________________.
3. If you invent something, it is an __________________.
4. If the moon is bright, it shines __________________.
5. If a car will not go fast, it will go __________________.
6. If you need a person very much, you __________________ on him or her.
7. If you plan to do something, you __________________ to do it.
8. If you had a fun time at a party, you might say you had a __________________ time.

☐ Correct

LESSON 12

A. New Words. Say each sound. Say each word.

1.	flew	paws	blew
2.	new	shrew	proof
3.	news	stream	drew
4.	threw	strewn	joys

5. A black crow flew over the wheat crop.
6. The shrew hid under the bush when the cat came into the yard.
7. I had a dream that I was on the news.
8. Who threw this red brick through the window?

B. Challenge Words. Say the words.

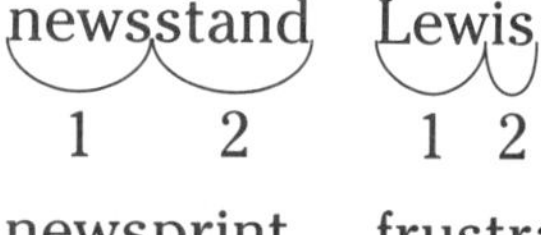

newsstand (1 2)	Lewis (1 2)	sewer (1 2)	dewdrop (1 2)	August (1 2)
newsprint (1 2)	frustrate (1 2)	classmates (1 2)	proofread (1 2)	appointment (1 2 3)

C. Word Parts. Say the words.

inspect expand badly windy

D. Words with Word Parts. Say the words.

1.	inform	extend	defeat	unreal
2.	snowy	hardly	plenty	darkness
3.	extinction	insightful	prediction	unhelpful

E. Sight Words. Say the words.

find	mind	kind		
over	give	told	other	another
through	want	all	about	many

F. **Passages.** Read each part of the story. Write the story part number under the picture that goes with each story part.

The Newsstand

Part 1

After school, Kris met with Beth and Liz at the new record store. "You did it, Kris,"
17 said Liz. "We are so happy for you!"
25 "Thank you," said Kris. "I can't wait to start my job as a news reporter. You were
42 right, Beth. A news reporter has to *find* the news rather than waiting for it to happen. I
60 have a plan that will help me be the best news reporter the school has had."

Part 2

76 Later that week, Kris went to see Mrs. Drew at the *Daily Free News*. "Mrs. Drew, " Kris
93 said, "I would like to join your news crew. I am a news reporter at school. I want to
112 report important news to my school. This is the best way to get up-to-date news."
127 "That's a smart plan," said Mrs. Drew. "I would like to have you work with my news
143 crew. But, I have another plan that may be more helpful to you." Kris's smile grew wide.

Part 3

160 Liz and Beth were jogging down Dew Street on Saturday morning when they saw Kris
175 standing in a corner newsstand. "Kris, what are you *doing*?" asked Beth.
187 "I am working for Mrs. Drew at the *Daily Free News*. I work at this newsstand selling
204 newspapers from all over each Saturday morning. Mrs. Drew said that I could read and
219 keep all the newspapers I want! You are speaking with one news reporter who will keep
235 the school newspaper up-to-date!"
239

_______________ _______________ _______________

G. Practice Activity 1. Read each question. Look back at the story on page 49. Fill in each blank with the best word.

Part 1

1. Where did Kris, Liz, and Beth meet after school?

   They met at the new ______ ______.

2. What did Kris have that would make him the best reporter the school had had?

   Kris had a ______ about how to be the best reporter.

Part 2

3. Who met with Kris later that week?

   Kris met with ______ ______.

4. Where was this meeting?

   The meeting was at the ______ ______ ______.

5. What did Kris want to join?

   Kris wanted to join the ______ ______.

Part 3

6. Where did Liz and Beth find Kris on Saturday morning?

   They found Kris standing in a corner ______ on ______ ______.

7. What did Kris get to keep from the newsstand?

   Kris got to keep all the ______ he wanted.

8. Why was Kris happy about working in the newsstand?

   Kris was happy because he can keep the school's ______ up-to-date.

☐ Correct

H. Practice Activity 2. Fill in each blank with the better word.

1. Jane got a ________________ at the ________________. — newsstand, newspaper
2. On a hot ________________ day, it is fun to go ________________. — sightseeing, August
3. Liz's ________________ went to the ________________ at 12:00. — lunchroom, classmates
4. The ________________ sells hammers and ________________. — screwdrivers, salesperson
5. ________________ likes to eat ________________ nuts and peanuts. — Lewis, cashew
6. When Lewis could not ________________ the top on the jar, he got very ________________. — frustrated, unscrew

☐ Correct

I. Practice Activity 3. Fill in each blank with the better word.

1. Barb will take a long time to draw the hawk. She will draw it ________________. — slowly, brightly
2. The crew will take the crates off the truck. The crew will ________________ the truck. — unpile, unload
3. Sam is very ill. He has a throat ________________. — infection, invitation
4. Mr. Martin will tell the children how to do the task. He will ________________ the directions. — extend, explain
5. Jan's soccer team will beat the High Kickers. Jan's team will ________________ the High Kickers. — defeat, demand
6. Jane never gets to class on time. Her ________________ upsets her teacher. — darkness, lateness
7. After dinner, Mark cleans the plates. His ________________ job is to clean the plates. — hardly, nightly
8. Liz has many socks. Liz has ________________ of socks. — oily, plenty

☐ Correct

☐ Checking Up

LESSON 13

■ **New Sound.** Say the word.

loud

A. **New Words.** Say each sound. Say each word.

1. out joint round
2. shawl cloud loose
3. house blew shout
4. proud blouse blown
5. She needs the round ball of string.
6. That cloud looks like a muffin.
7. The people will shout when they see the star player.
8. Fred was proud of his schoolwork.

B. **Challenge Words.** Say the words.

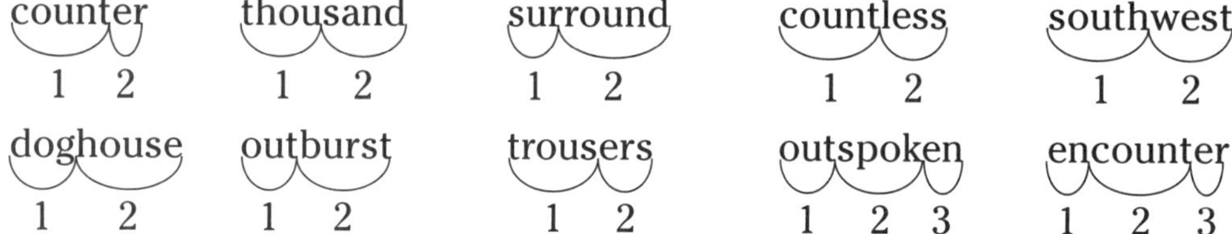

C. **Word Parts.** Say the words.

contain joyous

D. **Words with Word Parts.** Say the words.

1. consists expect inspect consider became results
2. famous attention tremendous simply useful nervous
3. construction explainable information disastrous

E. **Sight Words.** Say the words.

walk talk

coming woman even now kind

want about another cold some

F. **Passages.** Read each part of the story. Write the story part number under the picture that goes with each story part.

The Grant Ranch

Part 1

"I want to stop on the way back and see Mrs. Grant," Will said to his boy seated in
19 the wagon next to him. "I expect to have some time next week after the crops are all
37 picked. She may need some help," he said.
45 "Why would a woman live way out there on that ranch? The kids at school say they
62 have even seen her in trousers. She's kind of different, isn't she, Dad?" Tom asked.
77 Will grinned. "Nell Grant is an outspoken woman who works hard. That ranch is all
92 she has, and she considers it home. She's proud of her house, too. She is a widow and
110 her children are grown. She has worked hard to keep that old ranch. I think she has a
128 lot of backbone," he said with a smile.

Part 2

136 When they got to Mrs. Grant's ranch, she was sitting on the porch. Tom was
151 disappointed to see that she had on a blouse, skirt, and a shawl, not trousers. She greeted
168 them and asked them to join her for tea. They all went into the house and sat down.
186 "What's new, Nell?" Will asked. "I have some time next week if I could be useful
202 around here."
204 "Thanks, Will. I will keep that in mind, but right now I'm making out OK. I would have
222 a lot more time if that loudmouth Bob Drake would stop pestering me to sell out to
239 him. He wants that land on the southwest corner of the ranch. I have turned him down
256 a thousand times, but he keeps coming back." Then she grinned. "I think I stopped him
272 cold in his tracks today!" she said.

Part 3

279 "Have another cup of tea while I tell you about it," she said. "You will enjoy this. He
297 was sitting right where you are. I was paying attention, sort of. Then he told me he was
315 simply trying to help an old woman! I jumped up and shouted at him to leave. My
332 outburst surprised him, to say the least. I hope he stays lost for a while," Nell said.
349 She went to the window and looked out. "I hate to rush you off, but it looks like a
368 storm is brewing out there. You best go before you and Tom get soaked. Thanks for
384 stopping. I will see you soon."
390 They thanked her for the tea and left. It was starting to rain.
403

_______________ _______________ _______________

G. Practice Activity 1. Read each question. Look back at the story on page 53. Fill in each blank with the best word.

Part 1

1. Whom did Will and Tom visit?

   They visited ________________ ________________.

2. Why did the children think that Mrs. Grant was different?

   The children said that they had seen Mrs. Grant in ________________.

3. Why did Mrs. Grant have to work hard?

   She had to work hard to ________________ the old ranch.

Part 2

4. What did Mrs. Grant ask Tom and Will?

   She asked them to join her for ________________.

5. Why was Bob Drake pestering Mrs. Grant?

   Bob Drake wanted the ________________ corner of the ________________.

6. Did Nell sell the land to Bob Drake?

   No, she ________________ him down a thousand times.

Part 3

7. What did Nell do when Bob Drake said he was simply trying to help an old woman?

   Nell asked Bob Drake to ________________.

8. Why did Will and Tom have to leave?

   They had to leave because a ________________ was brewing.

[ ] Correct

H. Practice Activity 2. Fill in each blank with the better word.

1.	At the diner, Ann sat on a ________________ at the ________________.	counter stool
2.	Fred will ________________ his ________________ in the sink.	trousers launder
3.	The ________________ hid in the ________________ when the boys came.	doghouse raccoon
4.	More than a ________________ plants grew in the ________________.	thousand greenhouse
5.	Stacks of lumber ________________ the ________________.	sawmill surround
7.	There were ________________ newspapers stacked next to the ________________.	countless newsstand

☐ Correct

I. Practice Activity 3. Fill in each blank with the better word.

1.	There are three toys in the box. The box ________________ three toys.	contains consider
2.	Liz had lots of fun on her birthday. It was a ________________ time for Liz.	joyous disastrous
3.	All of the boys will be on the soccer team. The coach will ________________ all of the boys on the team.	include intend
4.	Tom will be home this afternoon. I ________________ him at 3:00 P.M.	expect extend
5.	For three weeks, Pam painted the farmhouse. She painted very ________________.	simply slowly
6.	Jan got 95 points on her test. She was pleased with the ________________.	results remake
7.	The noise grew in the classroom. The teacher said, "I need your ________________."	portion attention

☐ Correct

LESSON 14

A. New Words. Say each sound. Say each word.

1.	our	oil	sound
2.	cloud	claw	south
3.	ground	mouse	scoot
4.	moist	scout	hound

5. Our cabin sits beside a lake.
6. Pat plans to go south.
7. Clark planted grass seed in the ground.
8. The scout threw water on the campfire.

B. Challenge Words. Say the words.

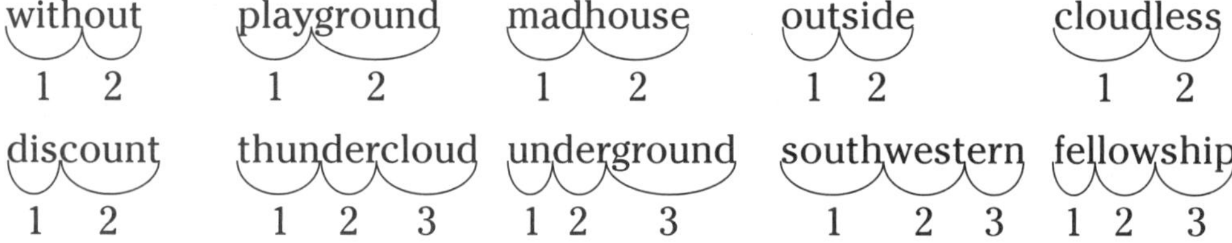

C. Word Parts. Say the words.

contain joyous

D. Words with Word Parts. Say the words.

1.	conduct	began	depends	details	distant	confess
2.	glamorous	happy	suddenly	horrendous	collection	lifeless
3.	predictable	connectable	interesting	returnable		

E. Sight Words. Say the words.

walk	talk			
warm	woman	even	over	kind
also	through	went	mother	give

F. Passages. Read each part of the story. Write the story part number under the picture that goes with each story part.

The Storm

Part 1

Will and Tom went south on Scout Trail. The rain was still light, but dark
15 thunderclouds were all around. The horse pawed the ground at the sound of the
29 distant thunder. "I hope we get home before those clouds burst," Tom said.
42 "We will do our best," Will said. "A lot depends on the horse and the rain. In the
60 meantime, what did you think of your encounter with Nell Grant?" he said.
73 "She is an interesting woman. I wish I had been a mouse in the room when she
90 shouted at Bob Drake." Suddenly, time ran out, and the storm was upon them.

Part 2

104 "You two are sopping wet!" Mother said as Will and Tom ran into the house. "Sit by the
122 fire and get warm. The storm came up fast. Did you stop to see Nell? How is she?" Mom
141 asked. They spoke of Nell Grant for a while. Will kept getting up to look out the window.
159 At last he said, "I can't help thinking about the crops and the livestock, too. This
175 storm is awful. Nell Grant's ranch will also be hit hard. Her barn is in bad shape. Wind
193 and rain like this could have disastrous results. Let's hope it stops soon. We may as
209 well go to bed. There will be a lot of work to do in the morning."

Part 3

225 When Will checked his land the next morning, things were not as bad as they could
241 have been. The roof of the barn was new, and that was a big help. Just before noon he
260 said, "I think I will ride over to see Mrs. Grant and her barn. Do you want to come,
279 Tom?" Tom nodded.
282 They rode around the back way, through the southwest corner of the Grant Ranch.
296 Will stopped suddenly. The old tool shed looked like it had sunk into the ground, and
312 Nell was sitting on the wet dirt by the shed.
322 Will and Tom rode closer. Nell turned to them and waved. "Oil. It's oil!" she said.
338 "That's why Bob Drake wanted this land! The storm did something to the ground. I am
354 going to be rich, Will! I can even get the barn fixed up right. Wait until I see Bob Drake,"
374 she said with a smile.
379

______ ______ ______

G. Practice Activity 1. Read each question. Look back at the story on page 57. Fill in each blank with the best word.

Part 1

1. Where did Will and Tom go when they left Mrs. Grant's ranch?

   They went south on ________ ________.

2. What did Tom hope?

   He hoped that they would get home before the ________ burst.

3. What did Tom say about Nell Grant?

   Tom said that she was an ________ woman.

Part 2

4. What did Tom and Will do when they got home?

   They sat down by the ________.

5. What was Will thinking about during the storm?

   Will was thinking about the ________ and the ________ and Mrs. Grant's barn.

Part 3

6. Where did Tom and Will go after checking the barn?

   They went to Mrs. Grant's ________.

7. Where was Mrs. Grant?

   Mrs. Grant was sitting on the wet ________ by the

   ________.

8. Why did Bob Drake want the land?

   He wanted the land because there was ________ in the ground.

☐ Correct

H. Practice Activity 2. Fill in each blank with the better word.

1.	The ____________ left ____________ the case of jewels.	without salesperson
2.	After ____________ class, the children went to the ____________.	playground drawing
3.	The ____________ smiled when she saw the ____________ sky.	cloudless farmer
4.	The subway went ____________ into a dark ____________.	underground tunnel
5.	The dark sky filled with ____________ of ____________.	thunderclouds thousands
6.	The ____________ gave a ____________ of $1.00 for each can of coffee.	discount storekeeper

☐ Correct

I. Practice Activity 3. Fill in each blank with the better word.

1.	Mrs. Smith is the leader of the band. She will ____________ the band tonight.	conduct consists
2.	Dennis was outstanding at tennis. He ____________ famous for his tennis.	began became
3.	Janet put on the new dress. She looked very ____________.	glamorous famous
4.	I think the criminal will tell about his crimes. I think he will ____________ his crimes.	confess contain
5.	I count on my mom's help. I ____________ on her.	detail depend
6.	The bike turned onto the highway next to a car. The car had to stop ____________.	brightly suddenly
7.	Troy has a thousand shells in his display case. He has a big ____________ of shells.	collection attention
8.	The rail went on and on. The trail was ____________.	lifeless endless

☐ Correct

LESSON 15

A. New Words. Say each sound. Say each word.

1. sprout coach couch
2. sprawl trout mouth
3. haul grouch spout
4. ouch threw flour
5. We sat down on our new couch.
6. Do you like fresh or frozen trout?
7. Turn off the bathtub spout.
8. "Ouch!" said Glen. "The horse nipped me."

B. Challenge Words. Say the words.

outgrew (1 2)

dismount (1 2)

farmhouse (1 2)

account (1 2)

countless (1 2)

Boy Scout (1 2)

outlaw (1 2)

scoutmaster (1 2 3)

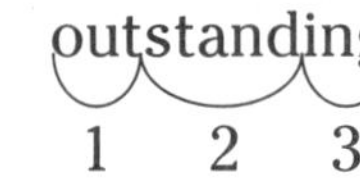
outstanding (1 2 3)

counterclockwise (1 2 3 4)

C. Word Parts. Say the words.

contain joyous

D. Words with Word Parts. Say the words.

1. connect invite describe result express contains
2. addition enormous directly reasonable nervous hungry
3. industry contrasting exactness prediction

E. Sight Words. Say the words.

walk talk

woman women over even warm

there told come many where

F. Passages. Read each part of the story. Write the story part number under the picture that goes with each story part.

The Lost Trout

Part 1

"I invited Ann and Mark over for dinner," Kris said to her husband. "Ann has the day off,
18 and her kids are at camp this week. They have not even seen our new house yet."
35 "That sounds fine, Kris," Don said. "While you show Ann the house, I can tell Mark
51 all about my fish. He will understand my disappointment. I just about had him, Kris.
66 That fish was enormous!"
70 "Don, you have told that old fish tale a thousand times this week! The fish gets bigger
87 each time you tell about it. At first it was just a trout. Soon you will be telling me it had
108 a spout like a whale!" Kris grinned and left the room to start dinner.

Part 2

122 Don sat for a while, thinking about the famous lost trout. Then he went into the next
139 room to find Kris. "OK, grouch, what can I do to help with dinner?" he asked with a smile.
158 "I have things well in hand," Kris said. "I will be happy if you simply clean off the couch
177 and put out the snacks. We still have time before Ann and Mark get here."
192 Kris set the plates and dishes on the counter and turned on the broiler. When she
208 went to find her husband, he was sprawled on the couch looking at a baseball game on
225 TV. She joined him until they saw Ann and Mark come up the driveway.

Part 3

239 They all chatted for a while, and then they went outside to see the yard. When they
256 went back in, Ann asked to see the rest of the new house. "Come with me, Ann," Kris said.
275 "I will take you around and show it to you. Besides, that will give Don some time to tell his
295 fish tale to Mark! He has been waiting for this all day," she said as they left the room.
314 Later, when Ann and Kris returned, Kris saw Don standing next to the couch. He was
330 holding his arms three feet apart. "I am glad I fixed beef, and not fish, for dinner," Kris
348 said with a grin. "I have had all the fish I can stand this week."
363

_______________ _______________ _______________

G. Practice Activity 1. Read each question. Look back at the story on page 61. Fill in each blank with the best word.

Part 1

1. Whom did Kris invite to dinner?

   Kris invited ________________ and ________________ to dinner.

2. What did Don want to tell Mark about?

   Don wanted to tell Mark about the ________________ that got away.

3. What happened to the fish each time Don told the tale?

   The fish got ________________ each time Don told the tale.

Part 2

4. What did Don do to help?

   He cleaned off the ________________ and put out the ________________.

5. What did Kris do?

   She set out the plates and dishes on the ________________.

6. What did Kris and Don do while they waited for Ann and Mark?

   They looked at a ________________ ________________ on TV.

Part 3

7. What did Don tell Mark?

   Don told Mark his ________________ ________________.

8. How long was the famous lost fish this time?

   Don's famous lost fish was ________________ feet long.

☐ Correct

H. Practice Activity 2. Fill in each blank with the better word.

1. Josh ________________ the green ________________ that he got for his third birthday. — trousers / outgrew
2. In the morning, the ________________ cleaned the ________________. — farmhouse / housekeeper
3. The Boy Scouts ________________ the ________________ up the trail. — followed / scoutmaster
4. There was much ________________ when the ________________ play ended. — outstanding / applause
5. The ________________ has to ________________ for each coin that she brings in. — salesperson / account
6. The gardener put the plants on the ________________ inside the ________________. — counter / greenhouse

☐ Correct

I. Practice Activity 3. Fill in each blank with the better word.

1. If a box has shells in it, the box ________________ shells. — connect / contains
2. If you ask people to your house, you ________________ them to your house. — invite / inspect
3. If you tell about something, you ________________ it. — describe / depends
4. If you want some food, you are ________________. — hungry / happy
5. If you tell about your feelings, you ________________ your feelings. — express / exactly
6. If you want to find the sum of three numbers, you should use ________________. — collection / addition
7. If something is very big, it is ________________. — joyous / enormous
8. If you have to do something fast, you do it ________________. — brightly / suddenly

☐ Correct ☐ Checking Up

LESSON 16

■ **New Sounds.** Say the words.

know phone quack write

A. New Words. Say each sound. Say each word.

1. knot wreck quit
2. knight phone knob
3. graph knife wrote
4. kneel quilt wrap
5. Little girls and boys could wreck a neat room.
6. Turn the knob slowly so it will not squeak.
7. Draw the graph on the paper.
8. Will you display your quilt at the quilt show this fall?

B. Challenge Words. Say the words.

dolphin	wrapper	jackknife	shipwreck	knapsack
1 2	1 2	1 2	1 2	1 2
knothole	vanquish	kneecap	underline	handwritten
1 2	1 2	1 2	1 2 3	1 2 3

C. Word Parts. Say the words.

complete handle

D. Words with Word Parts. Say the words.

1. command compose consult develop indeed beneath
2. simple middle title empty rapidly
3. completely connection considerable unscramble

E. Sight Words. Say the words.

don't	even	coming	find	two	sure
work	about	told	woman	give	machine

F. Passages. Read each part of the story. Write the story part number under the picture that goes with each story part.

The Time Machine

Part 1

"I am a nervous wreck, Trish!" Philip said as Trish reached for the knob. "This is the
17 third time this week you have made me go in there with you. If Quay finds out . . . I can't
36 even think about it!"
40 "I told you," Trish said, "that Quay is in her room on the phone. Besides, she thinks
57 we are outside. I think I know how to work it. I saw the notes Quay wrote. It's simple."
76 Trish looked at Philip in amazement. "Don't you understand? We give it the right
90 command, and it takes us back in time. Just think what we can see and do. You can
108 even pick the first date."

Part 2

113 "Are you nuts?" Philip yelled. "We don't even know if it works or not! For all you
130 know, this time machine will split us into thousands of bits and even Quay will not
146 know how to unscramble our parts."
152 "For your information," Trish said, "I *know* it works fine. Quay keeps detailed notes.
166 Last week she sent a knife way back to 1939. It came back with a flick of Quay's wrist!
185 The machine is completely safe."
190 Philip looked stunned. "A knife? Big deal! You want me to risk *my* life because a knife
207 came back? Why do you think she is keeping this time machine under wraps? She still
223 is not sure how it will work with *people*."

Part 3

232 "I have faith in Quay," Trish said. "Besides, I want to be the first woman to travel
249 back in time. I also know just where I want to go. I long to have a knight kneel at my feet
271 and kiss my hand." Trish giggled.
277 Philip and Trish discussed the time machine some more. At last, Trish said, "I
291 understand how you feel, Philip, but I am willing to risk it. I will try it first. If I return
311 safely, will you go with me next time?"
319 Philip said he would. Trish turned some knobs and consulted Quay's notes. Then
332 with a knot in her throat, she said, "Wish me luck!"
343

__________ __________ __________

G. Practice Activity 1. Read each question. Look back at the story on page 65. Fill in each blank with the best word.

Part 1

1. Who wanted to look at the time machine?

   ____________________ wanted to look at the time machine.

2. Whom did the time machine belong to?

   The time machine belonged to ____________________.

3. What is Trish letting Philip do?

   Trish is letting Philip pick the first ____________________.

Part 2

4. Why did Trish think the time machine would work?

   Last week Quay had sent a ____________________ back to 1939.

5. Why was Philip not sure that the time machine was safe?

   Philip was not sure how it would work with ____________________.

Part 3

6. Why did Trish want to go back in time?

   She wanted a ____________________ to kiss her hand.

7. Who was going to take the first ride in the time machine?

   ____________________ was going to take the first ride.

8. What did Trish say after she turned some knobs in the time machine?

   She said, "____________________ ____________________ ____________________!"

☐ Correct

H. Practice Activity 2. Fill in each blank with the better word.

knapsack **jackknife** **shipwreck** **underline**
wrapper **handwritten** **knothole** **farmhouse**

1. The ________________ happened a mile off the coastline.
2. The ________________ came off the box.
3. The Boy Scout put his ________________ in his knapsack before the hike.
4. The reporter put his notepad in his ________________.
5. Jean looked into the ________________ in the tree.
6. The ________________ stood on a hill surrounded by trees.
7. Barb will ________________ the best words on the assignment.
8. The letter was ________________.

☐ Correct

I. Practice Activity 3. Fill in each blank with the better word.

1. If you make film into prints, you ________________ the film. — defrost / develop
2. If you finish a task, you ________________ the task. — command / complete
3. If you do something very fast, you do it ________________. — rapidly / slowly
4. If you make lots of noise, you are ________________. — empty / noisy
5. If you are a member of a club, you ________________ to the club. — beneath / belong
6. If a person is in front of you and a person is in back of you, you are in the ________________. — middle / simple
7. If you are very happy about something, you might be ________________. — joyful / helpful
8. If you plug in a cord, you ________________ the cord. — connect / confess

☐ Correct

LESSON 17

A. New Words. Say each sound. Say each word.

1.	phone	quest	phase
2.	quiz	math	wring
3.	phrase	quake	quote
4.	quite	write	knit

5. Paul's quest for fun never seems to end.
6. Be careful when you wring out your socks.
7. Tell me how to write a phrase.
8. Will you knit me some mittens for this winter?

B. Challenge Words. Say the words.

gopher 1 2	knapsack 1 2	quiver 1 2	orphan 1 2	shipwreck 1 2
knockout 1 2	banquet 1 2	wrinkle 1 2	emphasis 1 2 3	equipment 1 2 3

C. Word Parts. Say the words.

complete handle

D. Words with Word Parts. Say the words.

1.	combine	compass	condense	convict	define
2.	article	bottle	riddle	factory	correctly
3.	example	condition	comfortable	perfection	

E. Sight Words. Say the words.

sure	don't	care	even	two
were	should	about	put	others

F. Passages. Read each part of the story. Write the story part number under the picture that goes with each story part.

Phase One

Part 1

Trish sat in the launch seat. She checked all the knobs again to make sure they were
17 set correctly. Then, with a smile for Philip, she pressed the red button. The machine
32 made a loud sound, and Trish was no longer there.
42 Philip was quite shaken. He felt a quiver run up and down his spine. He felt sure he
60 would not see Trish again. "I should have stopped her," he said to himself sadly, "even
76 if I had to sit on her to do it. What will I say to Quay?" he sighed.
94 Then someone said, "What will you say to Quay about what?"

Part 2

105 Philip spun around quickly to see who had spoken. "Trish!" he squeaked. "You came
119 back! Or did you even leave?" He ran to the launch seat and hugged her with glee.
136 "I am surprised you are still waiting," Trish said. "Let's go before Quay comes in and
152 finds us. I sure have a lot to tell you." Trish shut the time machine off and put back
171 Quay's notes and graphs.
175 "What do you mean that you are surprised that I am still waiting?" Philip asked as they
192 left the room. "You left and came back in a flash. There was hardly time for me to sit down."

Part 3

212 Trish and Philip went into the game room. Trish looked puzzled. "Philip, I spent all
227 day in the past. Are you trying to be funny?" They discussed the time, but each was
244 sure about how long Trish had been missing.
252 "I don't know how to explain it," Philip said. "I am not even sure I care to. Just tell me
272 what happened to you."
276 "When I hit the button, there was light all around me. Then I must have fainted.
292 If my math is right, when I woke up, I was in the 1300s. I was sitting on the grass by a
314 big barn. I stayed there awhile and then I looked around. I don't think people could see
331 me because no one spoke to me. By the way, finding my knight is easier said than done.
349 All I saw were shopkeepers. I hit the wrist button and came back."
362

______ ______ ______

G. Practice Activity 1. Read each question. Look back at the story on page 69. Fill in each blank with the best word.

Part 1

1. Where did Trish sit?

   She sat in the ____________ ____________.

2. What did she press?

   She pressed a ____________ ____________.

3. What happened when Trish pressed the button?

   The machine made a loud ____________, and Trish was no longer there.

Part 2

4. What did Philip do when Trish returned?

   He ran to the launch seat and ____________ her.

5. How fast did Trish come back?

   She came back in a ____________.

Part 3

6. How long did Trish say she had been in the past?

   She said she had been in the past all ____________.

7. Where was Trish when she woke up?

   She was sitting on the grass by a big ____________.

8. Why did Trish think that people could not see her?

   No one ____________ to Trish.

☐ Correct

H. Practice Activity 2. Fill in each blank with the better word.

1. ____________ is Tom's pet ____________. — Digger / gopher

2. The ____________ saw a ____________ swimming in the sea. — dolphin / fisherman

3. The ____________ was a surprise for the ____________. — banquet / housekeeper

4. The ____________ in 1916 happened right off the ____________. — seacoast / shipwreck

5. The ____________ put his ____________ on his back. — knapsack / scoutmaster

6. Beth's ____________ was ____________ in ink. — assignment / handwritten

☐ Correct

I. Practice Activity 3. Fill in each blank with the better word.

1. Jan will finish her math quiz. Jan will ____________ her quiz. — complete / combine

2. Pete will tell about his trip. He will ____________ his trip. — define / describe

3. Janis will join the dots on the graph. She will ____________ the dots. — convict / connect

4. Barb will stay in the classroom. She will ____________ there. — remain / remake

5. The jar was filled with milk. The ____________ was filled with milk. — handle / bottle

6. Pam has many dresses. She has ____________ of dresses. — plenty / factory

7. Dan got the math problem right. He did it ____________. — correctly / directly

8. The factory was very big. The factory was ____________. — enormous / joyous

☐ Correct

LESSON 18

A. New Words. Say each new sound. Say each word.

1.	know	phone	wrench
2.	quit	knife	wrung
3.	wrist	thick	quick
4.	knew	sphinx	knelt

5. Did Jan know the locker combination?
6. Will you quit your night job?
7. Turn your wrist this way when you hit the ball.
8. Ed went on a trip to the Sphinx.

B. Challenge Words. Say the words.

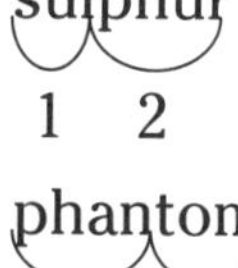

sulphur 1 2	playwright 1 2	unknown 1 2	liquid 1 2	knuckle 1 2
phantom 1 2	writer 1 2	tranquil 1 2	squirrel 1 2	sophomore 1 2 3

C. Word Parts. Say the words.

complete handle

D. Words with Word Parts. Say the words.

1.	commit	involve	explore	complain	confine	become
2.	terrible	safely	daily	readable	possible	twenty
3.	company	remember	combustion	containing		

E. Sight Words. Say the words.

sure	only	again	hold	about
your	also	give	want	would

F. Passages. Read each part of the story. Write the story part number under the picture that goes with each story part.

Into the Unknown

Part 1

For days, all Trish spoke of was wanting to go into the past again. "If you only knew how
19 tremendous it was, you would be begging to go!" she said to Philip. "You also must
35 remember you told me you would go with me if I came back safely. I did! Start thinking
53 about a time you would like to explore." Philip would still not commit himself.
67 At last one day, Philip said, "I give up. You win, but I have one condition to make. This
86 will be the last trip we take without telling Quay. For all you know, there may be something
104 important we are not doing, and your first safe return was just luck. Is it a deal?"
121 "OK," Trish said, "but let's go quickly."

Part 2

128 They went to the room that housed the time machine. They knocked first to make
143 sure Quay was not in the room. When they went in, Trish asked Philip where he
159 wanted the time machine to take them.
166 "We are going to see the Sphinx and check out her riddle," Philip said. Trish started to
183 speak, but Philip said, "Wait. I know people say that the Sphinx was a phantom and that
200 she was not real. As the story goes, she would ask people a riddle. If they did not answer it
220 right, she killed them. First of all, if the Sphinx is real, she cannot kill us. Besides, all the
239 time machine knows is what we tell it. If there was no real Sphinx, the machine should take
257 us to the Sphinx carved in rock on the Nile River. It cannot hurt to try."

Part 3

273 Philip wrote "SPHINX" on the screen while Trish set the buttons on the panel. Then
288 they put on the wristbands that would make them return. They sat in the launch seat;
304 Philip hit the start button, and with a quick thrust they were off!
317 They woke up on the banks of the Nile. There was the Sphinx—carved in rock. It was
335 cool and tranquil, and the Sphinx was a sight to behold. After a while, they knew it was
353 time to return. Back in the time-machine room again, they turned the machine off. Then
368 Philip said, "Keep me company while I tell Quay her machine works."
380 "Not me!" Trish said. "Telling Quay was your condition, not mine. Besides, it's going
394 to be hard enough to explain to a robot that we just wanted to explore the past."
411

__________ __________ __________

G. Practice Activity 1. Read each question. Look back at the story on page 73. Fill in each blank with the best word.

Part 1

1. What did Trish want to do?

   Trish wanted to go into the __________________ again.

2. What did Philip insist on when he agreed to go into the past?

   Philip insisted that they tell __________________ about the trip when they returned.

Part 2

3. Why did they knock before they went into the room with the time machine?

   They knocked first to make sure __________________ was not in the room.

4. What did Philip want to see?

   Philip wanted to see the __________________.

Part 3

5. What did Philip write on the screen?

   He wrote "__________________" on the screen.

6. Where did they wake up?

   They woke up on the banks of the __________________ River.

7. What was the Sphinx?

   The Sphinx was __________________ __________________

   __________________ .

8. What was Quay?

   Quay was a __________________.

☐ Correct

H. Practice Activity 2. Read the story. Fill in the blank with the best word.

When the bike's wheel began to squeak, Liz knew that something was wrong. If she did not stop the bike, Liz knew she would have a wreck. Liz quickly steered her bike onto the grass. When the wheels hit the grass, Liz was quickly thrown off the bike. Liz was smart to make the wreck happen on the grass.

1. The bike's wheel began to ______________.
   squeak stop quit
2. Liz knew that something was ______________.
   wrist wreck wrong
3. Liz knew that she would have a ______________.
   wreck wrong wrung
4. Liz steered the bike onto the ______________.
   rose path grass
5. Liz was thrown off her ______________.
   wheel bike ground
6. Liz was smart to have the wreck happen on the ______________.
   phone grass road

☐ Correct

I. Practice Activity 3. Underline the endings that make sense.

1. Philip can ________.
   a. put liquid into the pitcher
   b. wipe off the water from his windows
   c. slip through a knothole in the wall
   d. read a pamphlet about growing plants
2. Lewis could ________.
   a. put a jackknife in his knapsack
   b. get into a knapsack
   c. see a dolphin in the sea
   d. run quickly through quicksand

☐ Correct ☐ Checking Up

LESSON 19

■ **New Sounds.** Say the words.

match bridge

A. New Words. Say each sound. Say each word.

1. dodge catch edge
2. sketch judge snatch
3. witch chase patch
4. itch lodge lock
5. Look out for the sharp edge of the table.
6. Tim will judge the art contest.
7. Pam put a patch on the tire that was leaking.
8. The bug bite on my hand is starting to itch.

B. Challenge Words. Say the words.

catcher 1 2	hodgepodge 1 2	pitcher 1 2	outstretch 1 2	hatchet 1 2
hitchhike 1 2	patchwork 1 2	kitchen 1 2	underneath 1 2 3	referee 1 2 3

C. Word Parts. Say the words.

provide smallest

D. Words with Word Parts. Say the words.

1. protect compass instant explain control promote
2. needle lowest position quickly sweetest party
3. discovery protection contraption production

E. Sight Words. Say the words.

only	most	does	again	sure	four
also	many	some	walk	another	hour

F. Passages. Read each part of the story. Write the story part number under the picture that goes with each story part.

Baseball

Part 1

At one time or another, most boys and girls play baseball when they are growing up.
16 Sometimes children play baseball at school, or they form teams to play after school or
31 on weekends. People who like the game a lot can even watch baseball games on TV.
47 Some boys grow up hoping to become a player on a team like the Cubs, the Mets, or
65 the Dodgers. Players on these teams are paid to play baseball. Only the very best
80 players are on these teams. The teams play each other to see which team is best.

Part 2

96 It takes a lot of skill and hard work to become an expert baseball player. Players
112 must judge when to try to hit the ball that the pitcher throws. If the batter misses three
130 times, the player is "out."
135 If a batter does not hit the ball, the catcher has to catch the pitched ball. This is
153 a harder task than it may seem. Some pitchers throw the ball so fast that it may travel
171 close to one hundred miles per hour. A catcher wears thick chest pads and a mask
187 for protection.

Part 3

189 The object of a baseball game is to get as many "runs" as possible. A run is scored by
208 a player running around the bases and crossing home plate. When a player hits a ball,
224 the players from the other team chase and catch the ball. If a player hits the ball out of
243 the ballpark, it is called a *home run*. If a ball hits the ground before a player can catch it,
263 the batter runs to first base.
269 A batter may also get to first base by getting a "walk." This means the pitcher threw four
287 balls that were out of reach for the batter. A pitcher who does not have good control of the
306 ball can get his team into a jam quickly by walking too many players around the bases.
323 Baseball is fun to watch and fun to play. There are also other ways to enjoy baseball,
340 as you will see.
344

______ ______ ______

G. Practice Activity 1. Read each question. Look back at the story on page 77. Fill in each blank with the best word.

Part 1

1. What sport do most boys and girls play at one time or another?

   Most boys and girls play ________________ at one time or another.

2. What do some boys hope to be?

   Some boys hope to become a ________________ on a team.

Part 2

3. What does it take to become a baseball player on a team?

   It takes a lot of ________________ and hard ________________.

4. What happens if the batter misses the ball three times?

   The batter is ________________.

5. Why is it hard for the catcher to catch some balls?

   Some balls travel close to ________________ ________________ miles per hour.

6. How is the catcher protected?

   The catcher wears thick chest pads and a ________________.

Part 3

7. What is the object of a baseball game?

   The object is to get as many ________________ as possible.

8. How can a batter get a "walk"?

   If the pitcher throws ________________ balls that are out of the batter's reach, the batter gets a "walk."

☐ Correct

H. Practice Activity 2. Read the story. Fill in each blank with the best word.

On a hot summer day, Jean went to the marsh to explore. As she stood next to the pond, a squeaking sound rose from the thick cattails. Without making a sound, Jean knelt down on the moist ground. Slowly she crept through the cattails on her knees. In front of Jean was a nest filled with five little wrens. Still on her knees, Jean crawled away from the wren nest.

1. Jean went to the marsh to ________________.
   explore squeak creep
2. A squeaking sound rose from the ________________.
   ground pond cattails
3. Jean knelt down on the moist ________________.
   ground cattails path
4. She crept through the cattails on her ________________.
   wrist arms knees
5. The nest was filled with five little ________________.
   wrongs wrecks wrens
6. Jean crawled away on her ________________.
   knees legs hands

☐ Correct

I. Practice Activity 3. Fill in each blank with the better word.

1. Miss Sanchez will give the children paper. She will ________________ the paper. — provide / protect
2. Carla finished the task quickly. Carla worked ________________. — rapidly / slowly
3. Robin will tell us the details of the plan. He will ________________ the plan. — explain / explode
4. We will think about the plan. We will ________________ the plan. — control / consider
5. The red berry was very sweet. It was the ________________ berry in the bunch. — sweetest / smallest
6. Last night Jean unloaded the truck. The truck is ________________. — empty / lucky

☐ Correct

LESSON 20

A. New Words. Say each sound. Say each word.

1. ridge   pitch   phone
2. know   grudge   quote
3. fudge   hatch   badge
4. match   wedge   path
5. Our ranch is just over the ridge.
6. I gave up my grudge when he said that he was sorry.
7. How many eggs do you think will hatch?
8. Do these green socks match my pants?

B. Challenge Words. Say the words.

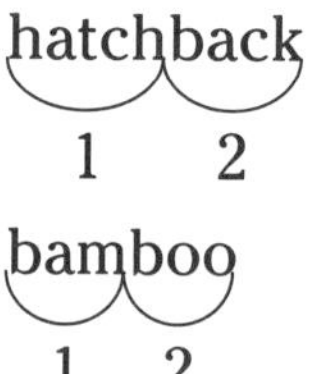

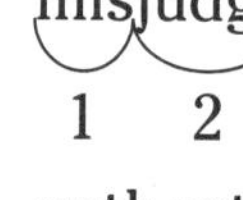

hatchback (1 2)   pitchfork (1 2)   misjudge (1 2)   phonics (1 2)

bamboo (1 2)   coastline (1 2)   authentic (1 2 3)   autograph (1 2 3)

C. Word Parts. Say the words.

provide   smallest

D. Words with Word Parts. Say the words.

1. program   unknown   retail   profile   exclaim   decrease
2. longest   awful   saddle   selection   fastest   gently
3. construction   considerable   propeller   forgetfulness

E. Sight Words. Say the words.

even   does   most   only   again

through   their   many   also   about

F. Passages. Read each part of the story. Write the story part number under the picture that goes with each story part.

Collectors

Part 1

Many people think of baseball as a game or a hobby. For thousands of people, on the
17 other hand, baseball is a job. While some people play baseball as a job, others *sell* to
34 fans things that are related to baseball. Fans will pay a lot for baseball bats, caps, mitts,
51 shirts, and pants. A baseball with the autograph of an important player can be sold for
67 a lot to a baseball collector. Baseball programs with autographs also sell well.
80 The fastest growing hobby related to baseball is collecting baseball cards. This is no
94 longer just a hobby for children—for many people, it is their life's work.

Part 2

108 Baseball-card collectors have to know a great deal about the game and all the
122 players. They keep track of all this information through baseball-card newsletters and
134 by talking to other collectors. They can do this on the phone or at meetings.
149 Some cards cost more than others. A baseball card that is printed with a mistake on
165 it, for example, is prized by collectors. All the collectors want to get one. When the
181 baseball-card company fixes the mistake, there will not be many like that card. A slight
196 ridge on a card, on the other hand, makes the card less important than other cards.
212 Collectors also keep track of which players are hitting, batting, or catching well.
225 Their baseball cards cost much more than those of unknown players.

Part 3

236 There is a lot of information about a player or a team on a baseball card. The card
254 shows a player and which team he plays with. It also has his position on the team, how
272 well he bats or pitches, and any other teams he may have played for. Each card also
289 has a number because it is part of a complete set of baseball cards.
303 Some companies make only baseball cards. The hobby is growing so quickly that a
317 considerable number of new companies have started to print baseball cards also.
329

____

____

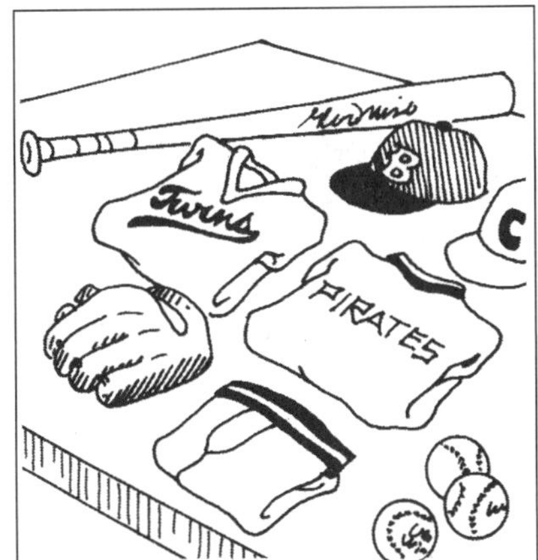

____

G. Practice Activity 1. Read each question. Look back at the story on page 81. Fill in each blank with the best word.

Part 1

1. What is the fastest growing hobby related to baseball?

   The fastest growing hobby related to baseball is ________________

   ________________ ________________.

2. Why do people collect baseball cards?

   People collect baseball cards as a hobby or their life's ________________.

Part 2

3. How do baseball-card collectors get information about baseball?

   They read baseball-card ________________ and talk to other

   ________________.

4. Why is a baseball card with a mistake prized by collectors?

   There will not be many cards like that ________________.

Part 3

5. What information is on a baseball card?

   A baseball card shows the player and tells which ________________ he plays with.

6. What other information is on a baseball card?

   The card tells the player's ________________ on the team and how well

   he ________________ or pitches.

7. Why does a baseball card have a number on it?

   The number shows that the card is part of a ________________ set of baseball cards.

8. Why would a new company want to make baseball cards?

   A new company might want to make baseball cards because the hobby is

   ________________ so quickly.

☐ Correct

H. Practice Activity 2. Fill in each blank with the better word.

1. People should not __________________ on the __________________. — hitchhike / highway
2. There was a __________________ at the __________________ game. — referee / basketball
3. The waitress put the plates __________________ the __________________. — underneath / counter
4. The __________________ was right off the __________________. — coastline / shipwreck
5. The __________________ told how to make a __________________ quilt. — patchwork / pamphlet
6. The __________________ was for the __________________ player. — saxophone / applause

☐ Correct

I. Practice Activity 3. Fill in each blank with the better word.

1. We saw a TV show. We saw a TV __________________. — program / provide
2. I do not know that girl. That girl is __________________ to me. — unwrap / unknown
3. Jeff is very short. He is the __________________ boy in the class. — longest / shortest
4. Mr. Martin will send three children to another room. The number of children in our classroom will __________________. — decrease / describe
5. Molly was very ill. Molly felt __________________. — useful / awful
6. The green scooter was very fast. It was the __________________ scooter on the road. — fastest / slowest
7. The yellow candle was very small. It was the __________________ candle on the birthday cake. — smallest / sweetest
8. Mark wrote a paper without a mistake. He wrote the paper __________________. — suddenly / correctly

☐ Correct

LESSON 21

A. New Words. Say each sound. Say each word.

1. hitch bridge switch
2. math nudge Mitch
3. ditch blotch budge
4. scratch swish latch
5. Switch seats with me, please.
6. Will you nudge Ned so he will wake up?
7. I can't get this blotch of paint out of my pants.
8. Release the latch so the dogs can go out.

B. Challenge Words. Say the words.

pitchfork drawbridge stretcher hopscotch

switchover graphite gopher yard line

C. Word Parts. Say the words.

provide smallest

D. Words with Word Parts. Say the words.

1. proclaim discuss require confuse combat profound
2. sharpest settle meanness safest closely station
3. container formation rejection playfulness progression

E. Sight Words. Say the words.

their only most even does

many also find some over

F. Passages. Read each part of the story. Write the story part number under the picture that goes with each story part.

Baseball Cards

Part 1

Boys and girls have been collecting baseball cards for a long time. Sometimes when
14 you get a pack of baseball cards, there are five different cards and a stick of bubble
31 gum. Many people like to collect cards of the players they like best. Some collectors try
47 to get cards for a whole team. Still others get all the cards for all the baseball players. A
66 set of all the players has close to 800 cards in it!
78 What can you do if you get more than one card for the same player? You can sell it or
98 trade it to another collector who needs that card. In baseball-card clubs, collectors
111 meet to sell, discuss, and trade cards. At these meetings, you may find old baseball
126 cards that cost a lot.

Part 2

131 Many old baseball cards are quite hard to find. Collectors may have discarded the cards
146 when the cards got old. Other collectors simply may have lost interest in collecting cards
161 and discarded their collections. Because old cards were thrown out, there are not too
175 many of them left. If you had some of these old baseball cards, you could become quite
192 rich very fast. There is just one hitch—the card must be in mint (like new) condition. A
210 scratch, a bent corner, or a printing blotch or smudge decreases how much a card is
226 worth. Collectors carefully inspect and judge the condition of old cards.

Part 3

237 If your mom and dad collected baseball cards when they were children, you might
251 see if you can find those cards. Look in old boxes or containers stored in the attic. This
269 may mean some digging, but it could also make you rich.
280 There are some remarkable cards to look for. A 1963 Pete Rose baseball card sells for
296 about $450. He played first base. You could also get $450 if you own a 1953 Willie Mays
314 card. He was known for his hitting and base-stealing. Ty Cobb had more hits than any
330 other man in baseball (4,191). His 1911 baseball card fetches about $500. Babe Ruth, a
345 left-handed New York player, was best known for hitting home runs. His 1911 baseball
359 card sells for $750. Last, but not least, there was a man named Honus Wagner, who
375 played between 1909 and 1911 as a shortstop. *His* baseball card, of which there are not
391 many, sells for over $20,000!
396

______________ ______________ ______________

G. Practice Activity 1. Read each question. Look back at the story on page 85. Fill in each blank with the best word or number.

Part 1

1. How many baseball cards do you get in a pack?

   Often the pack will have ____________________ cards.

2. What can you do if you have more than one card for the same player?

   You can ____________________ or ____________________ the card to another collector.

3. Where might you meet other baseball-card collectors?

   You might meet them at a meeting of a baseball-card ____________________.

Part 2

4. What kind of condition do old cards need to be in?

   The cards need to be in ____________________ (like new) condition.

5. What would make a card not in mint condition?

   A card would not be in mint condition if it had a ____________________ or a ____________________ corner.

Part 3

6. What does a Pete Rose baseball card sell for?

   A Pete Rose baseball card sells for about ____________________.

7. What was Willie Mays known for?

   Willie Mays was known for his ____________________ and for ____________________ bases.

8. What was Babe Ruth best known for?

   He was known for hitting ____________________ ____________________.

☐ Correct

H. Practice Activity 2. Read each list. Cross out the word that does not belong in each list.

1.	kitchen farmhouse bedroom bathroom	4.	coastline shipwreck harbor knapsack	7.	gopher badger baboon bamboo
2.	catcher hopscotch baseball pitcher	5.	pocketknife jackknife hatchet penknife	8	playground hopscotch soccer baseball
3.	sludge mud grass muck	6.	dolphin sister orphan salesperson	9.	hammer gopher ruler spade

☐ Correct

I. Practice Activity 3. Fill in each blank with the better word.

1. If something needs to be fixed, then you could ________________ it. — repair / remain
2. If we talk about a topic, we ________________ the topic. — discuss / disown
3. If a car goes very fast, it might be the ________________ car. — fastest / sharpest
4. If people come to a new land to stay, they ________________ in the new land. — handle / settle
5. If a person is very mean, he might be known for his ________________. — meanness / darkness
6. If a car was very fast, it would pass us ________________. — closely / quickly
7. If you wanted to take a train ride, you would go to the train ________________. — station / selection
8. If a rope was very long, it might be the ________________ rope. — longest / safest

☐ Correct ☐ Checking Up

LESSON 22

■ **New Sound.** Say the words.

cell peace

A. New Words. Say each sound. Say each word.

1.	cell	glance	stick
2.	cone	voice	twice
3.	clip	space	trick
4.	peace	came	cent

5. Mark will glance out the window during class.
6. I brush my teeth at least twice a day.
7. Would you rather explore space or the deep sea?
8. You need peace and quiet when you work.

B. Challenge Words. Say the words.

circus 1 2	canteen 1 2	blockade 1 2	cinder 1 2
absence 1 2	spacecraft 1 2	second 1 2	electric 1 2 3

C. Word Parts. Say the words.

about moment

D. Words with Word Parts. Say the words.

1.	agree	compound	profess	avoid	consent	exhibit
2.	statement	hottest	murderous	table	affection	government
3.	exploration	amazement	reflection	disposable	profession	unspeakable

E. Sight Words. Say the words.

every	their	does	only	sure
told	find	your	talk	again

F. Passages. Read each part of the story. Write the story part number under the picture that goes with each story part.

Lack of Funds

Part 1

Kay was walking home from school. As she drew close to an old oak tree, a voice said,
18 "Stop! I come from outer space. If you want to see what a spaceman looks like, pick up that
37 stick on the ground and tap the tree trunk twice. Do not be afraid. I come in peace."
55 "Joseph," Kay said, "you fooled me with that trick yesterday. Come out from your
69 hiding place." She glanced around and saw Joseph walking in her direction.
81 "I should have known it would not work a second time," Joseph admitted. "It sure
96 was fun when we saw the exciting space exhibit at the circus last week. I wish we could
114 go again."

Part 2

116 "I agree," Kay said. "I would like to go, too, but I don't see how I can. I spent every last cent
138 I had last week. It cost me fifty cents every time you made me go see the space exhibit.
157 Between that and the admission price, not to mention all the snacks, I am flat broke. I am
175 going to have to wait until the next time the circus comes before I can go again."
192 "I know what you mean," Joseph said. "My mom gave me a stern look when I asked
209 her about it last night. On the other hand, she did not say no, so there may still be a
229 chance. I will talk to her about it again and I will let you know what she says."

Part 3

247 Joseph got to the house before his mom came home. He quickly set the table—he
263 hoped that would make his mom happy. Then he went to his room to start his homework.
280 Later, as Joseph and his mom were eating dinner, he asked her if he could go to the
298 circus again. "Joseph," she said, "you have my consent. That's no problem, but you
312 must pay your own way. Last week you made the choice to spend all I gave you in one
331 night at the circus. If you want to go again, you will have to find a way to pay for it
352 yourself. The circus will be around for another two weeks. If you put your mind to the
369 task, I am sure you will think of something."
378 "OK, Mom, I will," he said. "I will talk to Kay and we will form a plan. See you later."
398

__________ __________ __________

G. Practice Activity 1. Read each question. Look back at the story on page 89. Fill in each blank with the best word.

Part 1

1. What did the voice tell Kay to do?

   The voice told Kay to tap the tree ____________________.

2. Who did the voice belong to?

   The voice belonged to ____________________.

3. What did Joseph want to see again?

   Joseph wanted to see the ____________________ exhibit at the circus.

Part 2

4. Why was Kay unable to go to the circus again?

   Kay had spent every last ____________________ she had last week.

5. How much did it cost to see the exciting space exhibit?

   It cost ____________________ cents to see the exciting space exhibit.

Part 3

6. What did Joseph do before his mother got home?

   Joseph set the ____________________ and started his ____________________.

7. What did Joseph's mother say when he asked to go to the circus again?

   She said that he could go, but he would have to ____________________ for it himself.

8. How long would the circus be around?

   The circus would be around for another ____________________

   ____________________.

☐ Correct

H. Practice Activity 2. Fill in each blank with the best word.

cents **twice** **voice** **cone** **space** **glanced** **peace** **sticks**

1. Josh ate an ice-cream __________________.
2. Tom's __________________ was very loud.
3. The rocket ship blasted off into __________________.
4. A stick of gum costs three __________________.
5. If you do something two times, you do it __________________.
6. Josh put ten more __________________ on the fire.
7. If we do not fight, we can have __________________.
8. Tom __________________ up from his work when a truck went by.

☐ Correct

I. Practice Activity 3. Read each list. Cross out the word or word pair that does not belong in each list.

1. alphabet, illustration, portrait, drawing
2. newspaper, newsstand, New York, newsperson
3. toothbrush, teaspoon, shampoo, toothpaste
4. outstanding, disposable, fantastic, terrific
5. classmates, schoolroom, spacecraft, classroom
6. thousand, seventeen, hundred, scarce
7. canteen, liquid, trousers, coffee
8. rocket, spacecraft, stretcher, launch pad
9. gopher, table, squirrel, raccoon

☐ Correct

LESSON 23

A. New Words. Say each sound. Say each word.

1. force mice cause
2. cinch place crow
3. since cape fence
4. cease crawl price
5. We let the mice live up in the loft in the hay.
6. Which place is yours?
7. Ron will paint the fence while Beth trims the bushes.
8. The price of gas will rise in the winter.

B. Challenge Words. Say the words.

cartwheel	center	embrace	cedar
1 2	1 2	1 2	1 2
pencil	kneecap	democrat	committee
1 2	1 2	1 2 3	1 2 3

C. Word Parts. Say the words.

about moment

D. Words with Word Parts. Say the words.

1. amount comprise prolong apart rewrite construct
2. enjoyment hopeful payment smartness perfectly history
3. apartment depression competition department

E. Sight Words. Say the words.

heard any every their don't

talk about some through there

F. Passages. Read each part of the story. Write the story part number under the picture that goes with each story part.

The Right Price

Part 1

The next day after school, Joseph talked to Kay about ways to make some fast cash. "It's no cinch to get an after-school job," Joseph said. "Besides, I might not get paid until after the circus has left. Do you know any place that needs a good worker and that also pays a high amount?"

"Well, that leaves out selling newspapers on a street corner," Kay said with a grin. "Shall we also scratch painting fences and digging ditches?" she teased. "OK, since you asked, there is one thing you seem to have overlooked. It was in the school newspaper. Don't you remember?"

Part 2

Joseph paused for a second and then said, "I have not seen the newspaper yet. What are you talking about?"

Kay reached for the newspaper. "Look," she said. "It says that the payment for handing out circus advertisements is a free ticket. For every two hundred ads you pass out, you get one free ticket. We could each do it and then we would get a ticket. I'm willing if you are. What do you say?"

"Two hundred houses is a lot of walking," Joseph complained. "We better go pick up the advertisements if we are going to go through with this." As they were leaving, Joseph said, "What a brain I am! I have the perfect plan! Let's go get the advertisements."

Part 3

On the way to get the circus advertisements, Joseph explained his plan. "We don't have to go to two hundred different *houses*," he said. "We only have to get them to two hundred different *people*. We can pass them out at those big apartment complexes on Cedar Street. It will hardly take any time at all, but it counts just the same," he said.

The next night, Kay and Joseph went to the circus again. They enjoyed seeing the horses prance around the ring and the other shows. They stopped for a moment by the space exhibit, but they did not go in. "Maybe next time," Kay said to Joseph as they left. "At least we got to come again, and the price was right!"

G. Practice Activity 1. Read each question. Look back at the story on page 93. Fill in each blank with the best word.

Part 1

1. What did Joseph want to get in order to earn some money?

   He wanted to get an after-school ____________ to earn some money.

2. Where did Joseph forget to look for a job?

   Joseph forgot to look in the school ____________.

Part 2

3. What kind of job did the school newspaper tell about?

   It told about a job handing out ____________ ____________.

4. How many advertisements did Joseph need to hand out in order to get a ticket to the circus?

   He needed to hand out ____________ ____________ advertisements.

Part 3

5. Whom did Kay and Joseph have to give the advertisements to?

   Kay and Joseph had to give the advertisements to two hundred different

   ____________.

6. Where did Joseph plan to hand out the advertisements?

   He planned to hand them out at the big ____________ ____________ on Cedar Street.

7. What did Kay and Joseph do the next night?

   They went to the ____________ again.

8. What did Kay say about the price of their circus tickets?

   She said that the price was ____________.

☐ Correct

H. Practice Activity 2. Read the story. Fill in each blank with the best word.

Cicero the Mouse said with a squeak, "Since it's dark, let's go to the barn. Maybe we can snatch some of Big Black's grain."

In a flash, the mice were off. They scampered over the bridge and down a path next to the fence. In an hour, they came to an open space. There stood the barn! Cicero did a cartwheel.

Inside the barn, the mice ran to the last stall. There they saw a bag of grain next to a pitchfork. In a second, the mice were eating the crunchy grain.

1. Where did Cicero want to go? Cicero wanted to go to the ________________.
   bridge barn fence
2. What did he want to snatch? He wanted to snatch some of Big Black's ________________.
   water grain hay
3. Where was the path? The path was next to the ________________.
   fence space bar
4. What did Cicero do when he saw the barn? Cicero did a ________________.
   bow cartwheel jump
5. Where in the barn did the mice find the bag of grain? The mice found the bag of grain in the ________________.
   hay place stall
6. What was next to the bag of grain? A ________________ was next to the bag of grain.
   someone pitchfork stall

☐ Correct

I. Practice Activity 3. Read each list. Cross out the word or word pair that does not belong in each list.

1. cartwheel
   somersault
   hopscotch
   committee
2. oak
   cedar
   coleslaw
   bamboo
4. pencil
   autograph
   democrat
   handwritten
5. hammer
   sawmill
   screwdriver
   wrench
7. portrait
   drawing
   embrace
   sketch pad
8. newsstand
   spaceman
   fisherman
   storekeeper

☐ Correct

LESSON 24

A. New Words. Say each sound. Say each word.

1.	prance	curb	couch
2.	cliff	cents	prince
3.	choice	crew	lace
4.	cool	nice	Rick

5. Make your horse prance through this part of the trail.
6. I am the prince in this year's play.
7. Do you like the white lace or the yellow lace?
8. She is such a nice person.

B. Challenge Words. Say the words.

citrus (1 2)	faucet (1 2)	playwright (1 2)	census (1 2)
boycott (1 2)	cloister (1 2)	civil (1 2)	countess (1 2)

C. Word Parts. Say the words.

about moment

D. Words with Word Parts. Say the words.

1.	asleep	respect	protons	among	concern	expect
2.	enjoyment	shapeless	mention	entertainment	partly	memory
3.	instruction	commitment	refreshment	glamorously	amusement	

E. Sight Words. Say the words.

any	every	their	don't	only
one	kind	another	from	walk

F. Passages. Read each part of the story. Write the story part number under the picture that goes with each story part.

First Snow

Part 1

It had been snowing off and on for three days. Rick was looking out the window. The
17 snow at the curb was close to two feet high. "Mom," he called, "may I go out and play? I
37 want to make a snowman. All the kids have one in their yards—all except me," he said.
55 His mom smiled, "Can't you think of some kind of entertainment that will keep you
70 dry? I am concerned that you may catch another cold." She looked at Rick's pleading
85 face. "OK, you may go out as long as you put on your hat, coat, boots, and mittens. Oh,
104 grab a scarf, too."
108 Rick ran to get his things while his mom sat at her desk. "Have a nice time," she said
127 as he went out.

Part 2

131 Outside, Rick began to pack the abundant snow into a big round ball. He looked up
147 and down the street, but no one whom he knew was outside. He had no choice—he
164 would have to make his snowman alone.
171 A little while later, Rick went into the house to look for a hat for his snowman. As he
190 came in, Prince wagged his tail and licked Rick's face. "Do you want to come out with
207 me and play in the snow, Prince?" he asked the puppy. Prince wagged his tail faster.
223 "Mom," Rick yelled, "Prince is going outside with me. Is that OK?"
235 Rick's mom turned from the desk and said, "I don't think Prince will like the snow,
251 Rick. He's still just a puppy, but you may try if you like."

Part 3

264 Rick and Prince went out. Rick walked down the steps into the yard and called to
280 Prince. Prince jumped down into a big snowdrift. He gave Rick a surprised look and then
296 just stayed perfectly still. He lifted one paw and set it back down. Then he lifted another
313 paw, but there was no dry place to put it. "Come on, Prince. Come here," Rick said.
330 Prince began to slowly walk toward Rick. Each step seemed to be in slow motion.
345 "Don't prance like a horse!" Rick giggled. "It's just snow!" As Prince came closer, Rick
360 saw that Prince looked unhappy. "OK, pal," Rick said, "let's go back in. We can try this
377 another day." Rick and Prince walked slowly back to the house.
388

______ ______ ______

G. **Practice Activity 1.** Read each question. Look back at the story on page 97. Fill in each blank with the best word.

Part 1

1. Why did Rick want to go outside?

   Rick wanted to make a __________________.

2. Why didn't Mom want Rick to go outside at first?

   She didn't want Rick to catch another __________________.

Part 2

3. Why did Rick have to make his snowman alone?

   He had to make the snowman alone because no one whom he knew was

   __________________.

4. Why did Rick go back into the house?

   He went inside to get a __________________ for his snowman.

5. Who wanted to play outside with Rick?

   __________________, Rick's puppy, wanted to play outside.

Part 3

6. When Prince jumped down into the snowdrift, what kind of look did he give Rick?

   Prince gave Rick a __________________ look.

7. How did Prince walk in the snow?

   Prince walked very slowly. Each step seemed to be in __________________

   __________________.

8. Why did Prince and Rick go back into the house?

   Prince did not like the snow. He looked very __________________.

☐ Correct

H. Practice Activity 2. Read each list. Cross out the word that does not belong in each list.

1. frustrate
   embarrass
   disappoint
   understand
2. playwright
   faucet
   drainpipe
   sewer
3. hermit
   kneecap
   pauper
   orphan
4. alphabet
   knapsack
   canteen
   jackknife
5. citrus
   cartwheel
   cedar
   cactus
6. spaceman
   circus
   arcade
   playground
7. charcoal
   saxophone
   sulphur
   graphite
8. pencil
   countess
   marker
   paper
9. lightning
   circus
   thundercloud
   monsoon

☐ Correct

I. Practice Activity 3. Fill in each blank with the better word.

1.	All of the children were ________________ ________________ for Mark.	asleep except
2.	Mom said, "Peg, wait a ________________. I will finish this ________________."	moment quickly
3.	There was a green bottle ________________ the ________________ red bottles.	among twenty
4.	The birthday ________________ gave Jim lots of ________________.	enjoyment party
5.	Linda has a very good ________________. She can ________________ lots of facts.	memory remember
6.	Tom and Barb could not ________________. Their ________________ went on all night.	disagreement agree
7.	The reporter has to ________________ her ________________ for the morning newspaper.	article rewrite
8.	The ________________ book had ________________ chapters.	twenty history

☐ Correct ☐ Checking Up

LESSON 25

■ **New Sound.** Say the words.

cage urge

A. New Words. Say each sound. Say each word.

1.	cringe	cage	gee
2.	gent	glee	merge
3.	gust	page	strange
4.	change	gate	gist

5. Gee! This batch of letters is wet.
6. Drive in the right lane if you want to merge.
7. The front page of a newspaper is exciting to read.
8. Put exact change into the slot.

B. Challenge Words. Say the words.

margin (1 2)	gently (1 2)	cabbage (1 2)	percent (1 2)
teenage (1 2)	sausage (1 2)	German (1 2)	grapevine (1 2)

C. Word Parts. Say the word.

reddish

D. Words with Word Parts. Say the words.

1.	atomic	detergent	replace	beside	prevent	increase
2.	punish	successful	embankment	homeless	education	publish
3.	repayment	recently	distraction	completeness		

E. Sight Words. Say the words.

father	year	their	every	again
even	two	many	others	through

F. Passages. Read each part of the story. Write the story part number under the picture that goes with each story part.

A Lesson from Europe

Part 1

Even as a little girl, Jane Addams could not understand why some people had so
15 much and others had so little. Jane was lucky. Her father was a very rich man and they
33 lived in a nice big house. When Jane and her father rode down the street in their buggy
51 in the 1860s, Jane would see children playing in the road. They did not have a yard or
69 lawn where they could play, as she did. Jane asked her father why this was so.
85 "I know it's hard to understand, Jane," said her father. "It may seem strange, but
100 some people just don't have as much as others. They work hard, but they are poor.
116 They cannot afford houses like ours."
122 Seeing poor children disturbed Jane. She decided she wanted to make a change.
135 When she grew up, she did just that.

Part 2

143 Jane's mother had passed away when Jane was just two. Six years later, her father
158 wed another woman. Jane got a new stepmother and stepbrother all at the same time.
173 Jane and her stepbrother, who was her age, became quite close over the years.
187 Not many women went to college in those days, but Jane Addams did. She wanted to
203 become a doctor and help poor people. Jane completed her basic college education,
216 but she did not become a doctor. She had terrible problems with her back. The doctors
232 treated her, but she had to stay in bed for a long time and could not complete her
250 advanced schooling. Although her dream of becoming a doctor was unobtainable, Jane
262 Addams still wanted to help poor people in some way. She only had to decide how.

Part 3

278 When Addams was feeling better, she went to Europe for two years with her stepmother.
293 When they returned, Addams knew for sure she could not go back to school again.
308 Jane Addams returned to Europe with a woman she knew well, Ellen Starr. While the two
324 women were in Europe, they visited a settlement house. This was a place where homeless
339 or hungry people could go for help. At last, Addams saw how she could help poor people.
356 Jane Addams and Ellen Starr discussed the settlement house they had seen in Europe.
370 Starr said she would like to help Addams start a settlement house. They returned home
385 and began to plan their own house, a place to help the poor.
398

______________ ______________ ______________

G. Practice Activity 1. Read each question. Look back at the story on page 101. Fill in each blank with the best word.

Part 1

1. What could Jane Addams not understand as a little girl?

   She could not understand why some people had so ____________ and others had so ____________.

2. What disturbed Jane?

   It disturbed Jane to see ____________ children who did not have a good place to play.

Part 2

3. What happened when Jane Addams was two years old?

   When Jane Addams was two years old, her ____________ passed away.

4. What did Jane Addams want to become?

   Jane Addams wanted to become a ____________ and help poor people.

5. Why didn't Jane Addams become a doctor?

   Jane Addams had terrible problems with her ____________. She had to stay in bed and could not finish her advanced schooling.

Part 3

6. Who returned to Europe with Jane Addams and visited a settlement house?

   Jane returned to Europe and visited a settlement house with

   ____________ ____________.

7. Who could go to the settlement house for help?

   ____________ or ____________ people could go to the settlement house for help.

8. What did Jane Addams and Ellen Starr decide to do?

   They decided to start a ____________ ____________.

☐ Correct

H. Practice Activity 2. Read each question. Underline the best words for each question.

1. Which words name animals?
   gopher baboon
   faucet squirrel
   pencil raccoon

2. Which words name people?
   sportsman faucet
   center spaceman
   fisherman inventor

3. Which words name ways of travel?
   subway train circus
   pencil scooter
   rocket seaplane

4. Which words name something to do with school?
   pencil sausage
   gaslight classroom
   alphabet homeroom

5. Which words name foods?
   cabbage oysters
   margin sausage
   coleslaw percent

6. Which words name body parts?
   elbow teeth
   kneecap cabbage
   kitchen cheekbone

7. Which words name tools?
   second circus
   screwdriver pitchfork
   hatchet hammer

8. Which words name something to do with water?
   center harbor
   faucet seacoast
   drawbridge countess

☐ Correct

I. Practice Activity 3. Fill in each blank with the better word.

1. The clay pot was red. It had a ________________ glaze. — reddish / punish
2. Jim and Mark will wash the dishes. First, they will fill the sink with with water and ________________. — decrease / detergent
3. Barb broke a dish. She will ________________ the dish. — replace / remain
4. Mark put the dish on the shelf next to the plant. He put the dish ________________ the plant. — beside / belong
5. The children go to school. They will get an ________________ in school. — education / station
6. The number of children at th school will get larger this year. The number of children will ________________. — indeed / increase

☐ Correct

LESSON 26

A. New Words. Say each sound. Say each word.

1.	germ	stage	gem
2.	age	glad	urge
3.	large	goose	grew
4.	drug	Gene	sponge

5. There is a rock-and-gem show in the city this week.
6. What is the age of your dog?
7. I would like a large serving of green beans, please.
8. Use a wet sponge to clean up that spill.

B. Challenge Words. Say the words.

ginger (1 2)	disgust (1 2)	target (1 2)	sagebrush (1 2)
greenhouse (1 2)	stagecoach (1 2)	Pacific (1 2 3)	gingersnap (1 2 3)

C. Word Parts. Say the word.

reddish

D. Words with Word Parts. Say the words.

1.	exercise	confirm	complete	agreed	proceed	alert
2.	furnish	wisest	torment	circle	attention	finish
3.	investment	helplessly	reduction	disrespectful		

E. Sight Words. Say the words.

father	year	care	women	any
their	talk	over	other	also

F. Passages. Read each part of the story. Write the story part number under the picture that goes with each story part.

Hull House of Chicago

Part 1

When Jane Addams and Ellen Starr returned to Chicago, they rented a large old
14 house called Hull House in a rundown part of Chicago. It was named Hull House
29 because some people named Hull had owned it many years before. Addams and Starr
43 then proceeded to clean, paint, and furnish the house. When they were finished, they
57 urged poor people to come to Hull House for help.
67 During the day, the people who worked at Hull House cared for children whose fathers
82 and mothers were at work. There were also clubs for school-age children to take part in
98 after school. At night, there were concerts and plays for poor people to attend.
112 Hull House was a good start, but Jane Addams wanted to do more.

Part 2

125 Jane Addams discovered a lot about poor people and their lives. She knew that many
140 changes had to be made so that their lives would be better.
152 Working conditions were terrible. Many children, like adults, worked long hard
163 hours. Addams worked to get laws changed to limit children's working hours and to
177 make working conditions better for all workers. She also knew that she could not make
192 all the changes alone.
196 During the next stage of her life, Jane Addams began to take on bigger projects. For
212 example, a huge concern of hers was that women could not vote. She joined with other
228 women to try to get the voting laws changed.

Part 3

237 With the help of many other brave women, Jane Addams helped women get the right
252 to vote in 1920. She also was the leader of the Women's Peace Party. This group wanted
269 people to talk about their problems rather than fight.
278 At the same time, Hull House continued to expand. People from all over came to see Hull
295 House. When these people returned home they began settlement houses like Hull House.
308 Jane Addams was also an author. She wrote *Twenty Years at Hull House*, which was
323 published in 1910. Some years later, in 1931, the Nobel Peace Prize was bestowed upon
338 Jane Addams. She had spent much of her life trying to make life better for many people.
355

G. **Practice Activity 1.** Read each question. Look back at the story on page 105. Fill in each blank with the best word or number.

Part 1

1. What did Jane Addams and Ellen Starr call their settlement house?

   They called it ________________ ________________.

2. What did the people at Hull House do during the day?

   They cared for ________________ while their fathers and mothers went to ________________.

Part 2

3. What laws concerning children did Jane Addams work to change?

   She worked to change laws to limit children's ________________ ________________.

4. What laws concerning women did Jane Addams work to change?

   She worked to change laws so that women could ________________.

Part 3

5. When did women get the right to vote?

   Women got the right to vote in ________________.

6. What party was Jane Addams a leader of?

   She was a leader of the Women's ________________ ________________.

7. What book did Jane Addams write?

   She wrote ________________ ________________ *at* ________________ ________________.

8. What prize did Jane Addams win for helping people?

   She won the ________________ ________________ ________________.

☐ Correct

H. Practice Activity 2. Read each story. Underline the endings that make sense.

1. The jeweler had a large display case in his store. In the display case were ________.
   a. large jewels
   b. lace dresses
   c. strange gems

2. The children wrote a play for the school. Gene was to be a prince in the play. On the day of the play, Gene ________.
   a. changed into his prince cloak
   b. got a sponge at the drugstore
   c. pranced onto the stage

3. The prince likes to ride his horse in the summer. One day the prince ________.
   a. rode along the fence to the bridge
   b. put a sponge in the bathtub
   c. rode out to the ridge

4. Gene works in a drugstore. He stands at the counter all day. One day Gene ________.
   a. crawled under the fence
   b. sold a sponge to Pete
   c. gave change to Beth

☐ Correct

I. Practice Activity 3. Read each question. Underline the best words for each question.

1. Which words name fun places?

arcade	dolphin
amusement park	circus
absence	playground

2. Which words name people?

teenager	democrats
August	hitchhikers
spacemen	catchers

3. Which words name numbers?

seventeen	thousand
hundred	thirteen
fifteen	center

4. Which words name things related to the sea?

harbor	saddle
cedar	seacoast
sagebrush	seashore

5. Which words name foods?

gingersnaps	radish
sausage	cabbage
stagecoach	gaslight

6. Which words name games?

hopscotch	ginger
finish	baseball
basketball	grapevines

7. Which words name plants?

citrus trees	sagebrush
cartwheels	greenhouse
oak trees	grapevines

8. Which words name ways to travel?

stagecoach	seaplane
sailboat	rubbish
scooter	subway

☐ Correct

LESSON 27

A. New Words. Say each sound. Say each word.

1. surge goose gist
2. green pages gash
3. bulge glee range
4. stage merge ranger
5. There was a surge of lightning during the storm.
6. Tape the torn pages of your book.
7. Please remove the teapot from the top of the range.
8. Gail plans to be a ranger in the fall.

B. Challenge Words. Say the words.

drugstore (1 2)	danger (1 2)	gateway (1 2)	carpool (1 2)
giraffe (1 2)	urgent (1 2)	congress (1 2)	autograph (1 2 3)

C. Word Parts. Say the word.

reddish

D. Words with Word Parts. Say the words.

1. afraid income excellent precede detect adopt
2. shipment rubbish thirty uncle tarnish nicest
3. instrument expression unafraid incorrectly

E. Sight Words. Say the words.

year	father	don't	give	does
many	hold	through	also	mind

F. Passages. Read each part of the story. Write the story part number under the picture that goes with each story part.

Dolphins

Part 1

Many people have seen dolphins on TV or in shows at amusement parks. They have
15 seen dolphins leap out of the surging sea or a large pool. We know many things about
32 dolphins, but we are still trying to discover more about them.
43 Some people think dolphins look like sharks because they are both gray, but there
57 are many differences. For example, a shark's tail moves from side to side while a
72 dolphin's tail moves up and down. Another big difference is the size of the brain. A
88 shark's brain is quite little; a dolphin's brain is as big as that of a fully grown person.
106 Dolphins seem to be very smart. Many people would like to know how smart
120 dolphins are.

Part 2

122 Dolphins like to play, so dolphin trainers teach them tricks that seem like play. When
137 the dolphin performs a trick, like jumping high out of the water, the trainer gives the
153 dolphin a treat as a reward. This is the way trainers teach dolphins. They give the
169 dolphins fish to eat when they want the dolphins to continue an action. The dolphin
184 soon knows what to do to get a fish. After a while, the dolphin becomes good at it and
203 does it for fun as well as for fish. However, if a dolphin does not want to do a trick, it
224 will not do it. Even a trainer cannot make a dolphin change its mind!

Part 3

238 There is another excellent way to teach dolphins—through the use of computers.
251 Dolphins talk to each other by making clicks and other sounds that travel through
265 the water. Through the use of a computer, a trainer's voice can be changed into dolphin
281 clicks and sounds. The trainer can then use the computer to talk to the dolphins and
297 tell them what to do. The sound travels through the water to the dolphins.
311 Dolphins have an excellent sense of hearing. They can detect sound at a long range.
326 If a trainer drops something small into the water that the dolphin cannot see, the
341 dolphin can swim right to it.
347 One of the nicest things about dolphins is their gentleness. Sometimes a dolphin will
361 even let a swimmer hold onto a fin and will give the swimmer a ride. Of course, the
379 swimmer should be certain that it is a dolphin and not a shark!
392

______ ______ ______

G. Practice Activity 1. Read each question. Look back at the story on page 109. Fill in each blank with the best word.

Part 1

1. What way does a shark's tail move?

   A shark's tail moves from ________________ to ________________.

2. What way does a dolphin's tail move?

   A dolphin's tail moves ________________ and ________________.

3. How is the shark's brain different from the dolphin's brain?

   The shark's brain is quite ________________, while the dolphin's brain is as ________________ as that of a man or woman.

Part 2

4. What do dolphins like to do?

   They like to ________________.

5. What do trainers do if they want the dolphins to continue an action?

   The trainers give the dolphins ________________ to eat.

Part 3

6. How do dolphins talk to each other?

   Dolphins talk to each other by making ________________ and other sounds.

7. How does the computer help the trainer talk to the dolphin?

   The computer changes the trainer's ________________ into dolphin ________________ and sounds.

8. What is one of the nicest things about dolphins?

   Dolphins are very ________________.

☐ Correct

H. Practice Activity 2. Read each story. Underline the endings that make sense.

1. Liz and Trish are planning to put on a play for their class. On Thursday, Liz and Trish _______.
   a. got up on the stage
   b. changed into their costumes
   c. put a goose into a cage

2. The housekeeper likes to keep the house very clean. This morning, the housekeeper __________.
   a. turned the pages in her newspaper
   b. cleaned the sink with a sponge
   c. killed the germs in the toilet

3. Mr. Perez went to the drug store. At the store, Mr. Perez __________.
   a. put a large sponge in his cart
   b. went up on the stage
   c. chose a green scratch pad

4. Ms. Sanchez went to the jewelry store. At the jewelry store, the jeweler __________.
   a. showed her a large gem
   b. urged her to get a new necklace
   c. showed her a sponge

☐ Correct

I. Practice Activity 3. Fill in each blank with the best word.

afraid	**excellent**	**shipment**	**thirty**
rubbish	**uncle**	**detect**	**adopt**

1. Barb did not like the gusty wind, thunder, or lightning. She was ____________________.
2. I ____________________ a note of sadness. Is something wrong?
3. This summer, Mark's aunt and ____________________ will come to visit.
4. Fred and Chris plan to ____________________ a girl and a boy. They want two children.
5. The attic is filled with ____________________. We need to throw it all in the trash.
6. The store got a large ____________________ of toys.
7. Mark did the math page correctly. On top of his page, the teacher wrote "____________________."
8. In September, there were twenty children in the class. By May, there were ____________________ children in the class.

☐ Correct ☐ Checking Up

LESSON 28

■ **New Sound.** Say the words.

down crowd

A. New Words. Say each sound. Say each word.

1. owl blown
2. flown plow
3. clown show
4. down crowd
5. I saw a large owl at the zoo.
6. All the birds have flown south for the winter.
7. What time is the late show?
8. There was a large crowd at the fair.

B. Challenge Words. Say the words.

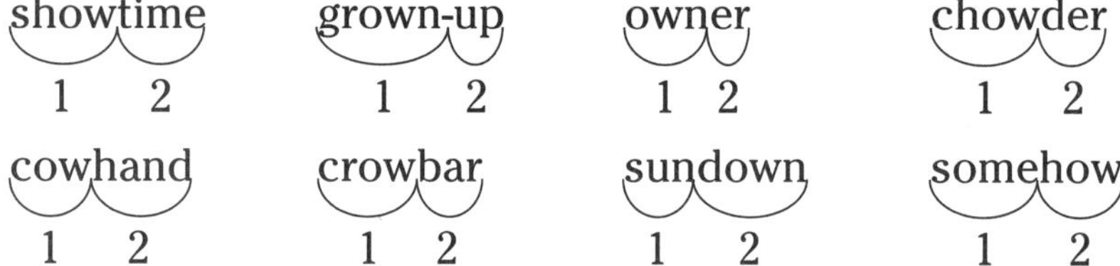

C. Word Parts. Say the word.

final

D. Words with Word Parts. Say the words.

1. adore proclaim condense demote exchange behave
2. normal furnish frankness generous gentle numeral
3. finally conversation naturally punishment

E. Sight Words. Say the words.

thought friend anyway someone somehow
were sure two their kind

F. Passages. Read each part of the story. Write the story part number under the picture that goes with each story part.

Planning a Talent Show

Part 1

"This talent show is more work than I thought it would be," Penny said to Ted. "I
17 thought all I would have to do is judge the acts on stage and proclaim the winner. Here
35 I am trying to decide how many clown acts and singing cowboys we can use. I also
52 have to talk Ms. Downs into printing the tickets for a low price and find someone to
69 work the lights. I sure could use your assistance, Ted."
79 "I don't know exactly what I can do, Penny," Ted said, "but I will help any way I can.
98 Ms. Downs is the owner of Showtime, the store on Page Street, right? If you want, I will
116 have a conversation with her after school. Maybe I can convince her to print the tickets
132 at a good price. After all, it is for a good cause."

Part 2

144 At Penny's house later, Ted said, "Well, the ticket problem is solved. At first, Ms. Downs
160 turned me down. Finally, I explained that the talent show was to raise funds for the school
177 band. Then she said she adored our plans and became quite generous. She agreed to print
193 the tickets for free! Somehow I think it had something to do with the fact that her uncle
211 conducts the band," he said grinning. "Anyway, what's next on the list?"
223 Penny looked down at her list. "We still need someone to sell the tickets, someone to
239 show people to their seats, someone to work the lights, and a clean-up crew for after
255 the show. Those are the main tasks," she said.
264 "I will talk to our friends at school," Ted said. "Between the two of us, we should be
282 able to find people for all those jobs."

Part 3

290 The night of the talent show was approaching. Penny had decided to set a limit of
306 two for each kind of act. As she explained to Ted, "We cannot have five clown acts. The
324 crowd will simply not enjoy the show. There must be someone out there who can
339 juggle or dance or something." Then Penny asked Ted how the ticket sales were going.
354 "It seems a little slow," Ted said, "but it's hard to tell. I think most of the people are
373 waiting to get their tickets on the night of the show. You just keep working on the show
391 itself. I am sure we will have a big crowd."
401

_______________ _______________ _______________

G. Practice Activity 1. Read each question. Look back at the story on page 113. Fill in each blank with the best word.

Part 1

1. What is Penny planning?

   Penny is planning a ____________ ____________.

2. Who did Penny ask to help with the talent show?

   Penny asked ____________ to help with the talent show.

3. What did Ted say that he would do?

   He said that he would talk with ____________ ____________ and try to convince her to print the ____________ for a good price.

Part 2

4. Why did Ms. Downs decide to print the tickets for free?

   She decided to print the tickets for free because the talent show would raise funds for the ____________ ____________.

5. What did Penny need people to help her with?

   She needed someone to sell ____________, someone to work the ____________, a ____________-____________ crew, and someone to show people to their ____________.

6. Whom was Ted going to ask to help with the talent show?

   Ted was going to ask their ____________ at school to help with the talent show.

Part 3

7. How many acts of each kind did Penny decide to have?

   She decided to set a limit of ____________ for each kind of act.

8. When did Ted think people would get their tickets?

   He thought they would get their tickets on the ____________ of the show.

☐ Correct

H. Practice Activity 2. Read each story. Underline the endings that make sense.

1. At the zoo, the crowd looked at many animals. The crowd saw ________.
   a. an owl in a cage
   b. a clown on a stage
   c. a baboon by a stream
2. At the circus, the crowd saw many things. They saw ________.
   a. a horse prance around the ring
   b. a farmer plow his crops
   c. a clown doing tricks
3. The farmer works hard on his farm. The farmer ________.
   a. plows the soil before he plants his crops
   b. cuts down the weeds that grow among his plants
   c. sees a clown at the circus
4. The clowns in the circus do many funny things. The clowns ________.
   a. show the crowd tricks
   b. read the pages of a newspaper
   c. dance and prance around the circus stage

☐ Correct

I. Practice Activity 3. Read each list. Cross out the word or word pair that does not belong in each list.

1. screwdriver, crowbar, chowder, hammer
2. grown-up, somehow, teenager, preschooler
3. sundown, morning, sunup, engine
4. sundown, cowhand, jeweler, salesperson
5. chowder, gingersnaps, cabbage, grown-up
6. giraffe, congress, baboon, raccoon
7. sausage, gingersnaps, hamburger, committee
8. spaceman, rocket, launch pad, showtime
9. stagecoach, crowbar, seaplane, sailboat

☐ Correct

LESSON 29

A. New Words. Say each sound. Say each word.

1. frown brow
2. growl slow
3. growth bowl
4. shown brown
5. Her frown disappeared when she saw the teddy bear.
6. I am a slow driver.
7. The growth rate of the eagle is astonishing!
8. Your brown shoes look good with that outfit.

B. Challenge Words. Say the words.

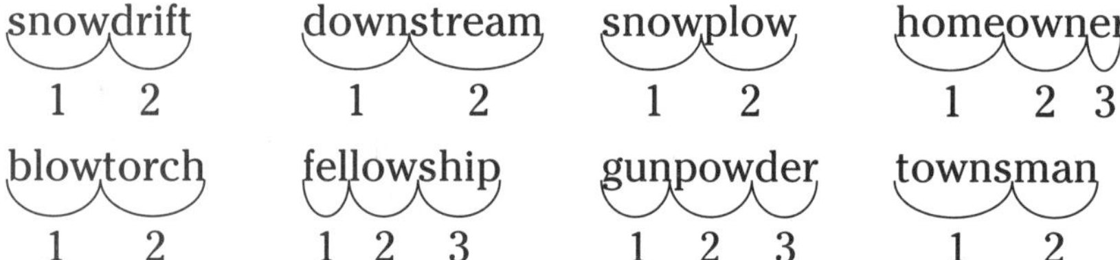

C. Word Parts. Say the word.

final

D. Words with Word Parts. Say the words.

1. prevail excuse await distant continue alarm
2. mineral numerous cattle swiftly pigment several
3. consumer expression expandable informally

E. Sight Words. Say the words.

thought someone friend only any

their care over sure don't

F. Passages. Read each part of the story. Write the story part number under the picture that goes with each story part.

The Show Must Go On

Part 1

Ted and Penny were sitting in the dining room at Ted's house. They were discussing the final plans for tonight's talent show. "OK, Penny," Ted said, "let's go through your list again. You have been frowning for two days now. Relax, will you? We have things under control. I got my friends to agree to take care of all the things you said you needed. I wish I knew what you're so concerned about."

"It's hard to explain, Ted," Penny said. "I just have this feeling. Several things could go wrong, you know."

"It's silly to waste your time thinking about what might happen," Ted said. "If you keep this up, you will be the only one who will not enjoy the show. Let's go back to your list and check it again. That should help."

Part 2

Later that afternoon, Penny got a phone call at home. It was from Ms. Brown, the school nurse. "I am afraid I have some bad news for you, Penny," Ms. Brown said. "I cannot be one of the judges for the talent show tonight. My little boy is ill, and I don't want to leave him alone. I am sure you can find someone to take my place," she continued. Penny told her she would and thanked her for calling. Then she phoned Ted.

"Don't be alarmed," Ted said. "I will find someone. You just meet me at school around six as we agreed. I will bring the new judge with me."

Part 3

At 6:15 that night, Penny still had not seen Ted. She had a grim look on her face. Finally, she saw him walk in with a tall woman in a brown overcoat. "Penny," Ted said, "this is Ms. Downs from Showtime. She has agreed to fill in as a judge. Will you show her where the judge's table is?" he asked. Penny did, and then walked back to talk with Ted.

"Thanks for all your help, Ted. I should have known you would not let me down. The show will be starting soon. Let's go find our seats. From now on, you and I will be just part of the crowd. Let's enjoy the show." They walked to their seats. Penny was finally smiling.

____

____

____

G. Practice Activity 1. Read each question. Look back at the story on page 117. Fill in each blank with the best word.

Part 1

1. Who was upset about the talent show?

   ____________________ was upset about the talent show.

2. How did Ted know that Penny was upset and nervous about the show?

   He saw that Penny had been ____________________ for two days.

3. What did Ted say that they should do?

   He said that they should check Penny's ____________________ again.

Part 2

4. Who called Penny and said that she could not be a judge?

   ____________________ ____________________ said that she could not be a judge.

5. Who said he would find a new judge?

   ____________________ said he would find a new judge.

Part 3

6. Why did Penny have a grim look on her face at 6:15?

   Penny had not seen ____________________ and the new judge.

7. Who had agreed to fill in as a judge?

   ____________________ ____________________ had agreed to be a judge.

8. How do you know that Penny was happy when the show began?

   Penny was finally ____________________.

☐ Correct

H. Practice Activity 2. Read each list. Cross out the word or word pair that does not belong in each list.

1. cowhand storekeeper giraffe grown-up	4. crowbar blowtorch sundown hatchet	7. rocket spaceman drugstore space ride
2. snowdrift snowplow snowman showtime	5. downstream townsman landowner homeowner	8. faucet sewer snowdrift drainpipe
3. sagebrush blowtorch cedar oak tree	6. stagecoach tractor snowplow homeowner	9. wrist kneecap elbow gunpowder

☐ Correct

I. Practice Activity 3. Fill in each blank with the best word.

final	**excused**	**continued**	**cattle**
alarm	**swiftly**	**several**	**asleep**

1. On the ranch, the cowhands raise __________________.
2. By 9:00, the children will be sound __________________.
3. The train was very fast. It __________________ passed the train station.
4. When the fire broke out, Jane pulled the fire __________________.
5. When the children finished their dinner, they asked to be __________________ from the table.
6. When the __________________ bell rang, the children sat down.
7. __________________ homeowners met at the town hall.
8. Jeff wanted to finish mowing the lawn. When the rain stopped, Jeff __________________ to mow the lawn.

☐ Correct

LESSON 30

A. New Words. Say each sound. Say each word.

1. flower crow
2. crown town
3. grow powder
4. gown glow
5. "Caw, caw," said the crow when it saw the piles of corn.
6. The queen is putting her crown on display this week.
7. Remember to get baby powder at the store.
8. The glow from the sun slowly faded as night approached.

B. Challenge Words. Say the words.

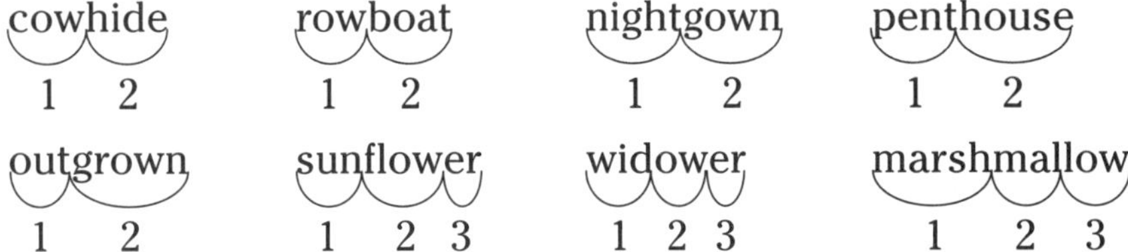

C. Word Parts. Say the word.

final

D. Words with Word Parts. Say the words.

1. preflight propose amend derail excite anew
2. hospital palest function struggle clearly mental
3. excitement unusual provision exactness

E. Sight Words. Say the words.

friend thought almost anyone every

over sure told another even

F. **Passages.** Read each part of the story. Write the story part number under the picture that goes with each story part.

Wedding Weekend

Part 1

Gale and Bob were walking home from school. "What did you think of that math quiz
16 today?" Gale asked.
19 "It was a struggle," Bob said, "but I think I did a good job. You know, Gale, I would
38 rather take another test than go home right now."
47 Gale gave her friend a look of surprise. "Clearly you are ill," Gale said. "Let me feel
64 your brow. Shall I take you directly to the hospital?" she joked. "You must admit that
80 was an unusual statement. Let's go over to my house, and you can tell me all about it."
98 They continued down the road to Gale's house.

Part 2

106 Gale and Bob went into the house and sat down in the den. Bob began to explain. "You
124 forget, Gale. This is the wedding weekend at my house. When Todd proposed to my sister,
140 Joan, I did not dream what a mess this wedding would turn into. I think my sister has
158 invited the entire town. Our house is filled with flowers and people from out of town. All
175 anyone talks about is wedding gowns or how the bride-to-be is glowing. My mother likes
190 the excitement. I even think my father is enjoying it. I just want it to be over so my life can
211 get back to normal. I even lost my bedroom to two of my uncles," he moaned.
227 Gale and Bob talked for a while. As Bob was leaving, Gale said, "Try to enjoy yourself.
244 Who knows? It might be fun. See you soon."

Part 3

253 The next day was bright and clear. Bob had to admit that it was a nice day for a
272 wedding. After he was dressed, he went to find Joan. Her room was filled with friends
288 helping her get dressed. He sat down and watched her put on her powder and lipstick.
304 Finally, his sister saw him and said, "You look handsome, Bob. Are you all set?" Bob
320 looked puzzled. Joan continued, "I am sure I told you that we want you to bring us our
338 rings. You are an important part of this wedding. This is a big day for all of us. It's
357 almost time to go." His sister gave him a big hug.
368 The wedding turned out to be nice for Bob after all.
379

_______________ _______________ _______________

G. Practice Activity 1. Read each question. Look back at the story on page 121. Fill in each blank with the best word.

Part 1

1. Where were Gale and Bob walking?

   They were walking ________________ from ________________.

2. What had happened in school that day?

   Gale and Bob had taken a ________________ ________________.

Part 2

3. Why didn't Bob want to go home?

   His sister's ________________ was this weekend.

4. Who liked all of the wedding excitement?

   Bob's ________________ liked the excitement.

5. Why did Bob want the wedding to be over?

   He wanted life to get back to ________________.

Part 3

6. What did Bob do after he got dressed for the wedding?

   He went to find ________________.

7. Who was helping Joan get dressed?

   Joan's ________________ were helping her get dressed.

8. What did Bob get to do in the wedding?

   He got to bring the ________________ to Joan and Todd.

☐ Correct

H. Practice Activity 2. Read each list. Cross out the word that does not belong in each list.

1. rowboat
   seaplane
   sagebrush
   stagecoach

2. townhouse
   penthouse
   nightgown
   apartment

3. jacket
   trousers
   sunflower
   nightgown

4. snowplow
   snowdrift
   showtime
   snowbank

5. widower
   penthouse
   landowner
   homeowner

6. cowhide
   stagecoach
   outgrown
   cowhand

7. grown-up
   teenager
   toddler
   sundown

8. sunflower
   rowboat
   sagebrush
   grapevine

9. marshmallow
   hamburger
   cowhide
   cabbage

☐ Correct

I. Practice Activity 3. Fill in each blank with the better word.

1. The girl was very pale. In fact, she was the ____________________ girl in the hospital. — palest / longest
2. When you are sick, you usually stay home. But if you are very sick, you might go to the ____________________. — hospital / unusual
3. Pam saw the owl in the distant trees. She could see the owl ____________________. — gently / clearly
4. Putting the toy train's track together was hard for Jeff. Jeff had to ____________________ to get the track together. — struggle / needle
5. The last train of the day left at 9:00. It was the ____________________ train of the day. — normal / final
6. The fire broke out at 6:00. At 6:15, the fire ____________________ sounded. — afraid / alarm
7. Many people came to the yard sale. ____________________ people came to the sale. — numerous / famous
8. The teacher did not like the way Jan acted in class. The teacher did not like how Jan ____________________ in class. — belonged / behaved

☐ Correct ☐ Checking Up

LESSON 31

■ **New Sound.** Say the words.

shook book

A. New Words. Say each sound. Say each word.

1. book shook
2. bloom cook
3. stood spool
4. fool foot
5. The excited speaker shook his fist at the crowd.
6. We will cook the peas and corn in the steamer.
7. Mark stood in the rain until the bus arrived.
8. Which foot belongs on the gas pedal?

B. Challenge Words. Say the words.

woodpile 1 2	football 1 2	scooter 1 2	wooden 1 2	teaspoon 1 2
moonlight 1 2	fishhook 1 2	mushroom 1 2	bookkeeper 1 2 3	footlocker 1 2 3

C. Word Parts. Say the word.

passive

D. Words with Word Parts. Say the words.

1.	adult	resale	predate	concept
2.	negative	shameful	punishable	attractive
3.	compliment	regretful	expertness	incentive
4.	retirement	complication	exceptional	insufferable

E. Sight Words. Say the words.

enough	learn	anything	thought	almost
only	don't	father	sure	does

F. Passages. Read each part of the story. Write the story part number under the picture that goes with each story part.

Cork from Portugal

Part 1

Norm was in the den looking at this father's books. His father was sitting nearby
15 reading the newspaper. After a while, Norm came over and stood by his father's chair.
30 "Dad," Norm said, "will you help me think of a topic for my report? I want to write
48 about something unusual, but I can't think of anything."
57 His father thought quietly for several moments, and then he said, "How about writing
71 a report on mushrooms or lighthouses or cork? Cork might be your best choice. Not
86 only is it an unusual topic, but your Uncle Gregg can tell you all about it. He worked on
105 a cork farm in Portugal, you know. Why don't you give him a call?"

Part 2

119 The next day after school, Norm went to visit his uncle. They talked for a while, and
136 then Norm said, "Uncle Gregg, I thought you were a retired bookkeeper. Dad said that
151 you worked on a cork farm in Portugal. Can you tell me enough about cork so that I can
170 write a report on it?"
175 "I am sure I can," Uncle Gregg said. "I worked on a cork farm most of my adult life. I only
196 worked as a bookkeeper here because there are no cork farms in this part of the country.
213 At times I still miss it. Well, sit there on that footstool and I will tell you all about cork."

Part 3

233 Uncle Gregg started by saying, "Most cork comes from the forests of Portugal. Cork
247 comes from one kind of oak tree. It takes a lot of training for a cork stripper to learn
266 how to strip cork from a tree without hurting the tree.
277 The first thing a cork stripper does is make two cuts in the tree bark. One is around
295 the top of the tree trunk and the other is at the bottom of the trunk. Then the stripper
314 makes a slice from the top to the bottom of the trunk. If the cork stripper has been
332 careful, the cork will now peel off the tree, just like taking off the skin of a banana."
350 Uncle Gregg stopped at this point and said, "Why don't we eat dinner. Then I will
366 continue to tell you about cork."
372

____

____

____

G. Practice Activity 1. Read each question. Look back at the story on page125. Fill in each blank with the best word.

Part 1

1. What did Norm want his dad to do?

   He wanted his dad to help him think of a ________________ for his ________________.

2. What did Norm want to write about?

   He wanted to write about something ________________.

3. Why did Norm's father suggest that Norm should call his uncle?

   Norm's father suggested that Norm should call Uncle ________________ because he knows a lot about ________________.

Part 2

4. Where did Norm go after school?

   Norm went to visit his ________________.

5. Where had Uncle Gregg worked during most of his adult life?

   He had worked on a ________________ ________________.

Part 3

6. Where does most cork come from?

   Most cork comes from the ________________ of ________________.

7. What is the first thing that a cork stripper does?

   The first thing that a cork stripper does is to make ________________ cuts in the ________________ ________________.

8. What does the cork stripper do next?

   The cork stripper makes a slice from the ________________ down to the ________________ of the trunk.

☐ Correct

H. Practice Activity 2. Read each list. Cross out the word that does not belong in each list.

1. woodpile
   sausage
   cabbage
   mushrooms

2. sunflower
   teaspoons
   sagebrush
   grapevines

3. penthouse
   playhouse
   stagecoach
   doghouse

4. bookkeeper
   snowplow
   widower
   homeowner

5. rowboat
   boathouse
   sailboat
   motorboat

6. scooter
   snowplow
   rowboat
   cowhide

7. football
   teaspoon
   basketball
   soccer

8. nightgown
   jacket
   trousers
   wooden

9. blowtorch
   crowbar
   mushroom
   hammer

☐ Correct

I. Practice Activity 3. Fill in each blank with the better word.

1. If you are a grown-up, you are an ____________________. — adopt / adult

2. If you stop something from happening, you ____________________ it. — prepay / prevent

3. If you did something that was wrong, it might be a ____________________ shameful thing to do. — shameful / cheerful

4. If you like someone very much, you might think that person is ____________________. — attractive / passive

5. If you went to the last track meet of the season, you would be at the ____________________ track meet. — final / mental

6. If something is very hard for you to do, you might have to ____________________ to finish it. — gentle / struggle

7. If you did something very fast, you would do it ____________________. — swiftly / nightly

8. If you don't stop working on something, you ____________________ working on it. — concept / continue

☐ Correct

LESSON 32

A. New Words. Say each sound. Say each word.

1. hood spool
2. hook crook
3. gloom good
4. brook boost
5. The hood of my pink raincoat is torn.
6. You can find your coat on the hook to the right of the door.
7. *Where the Red Fern Grows* is a good book.
8. Watch the deer leap over the brook.

B. Challenge Words. Say the words.

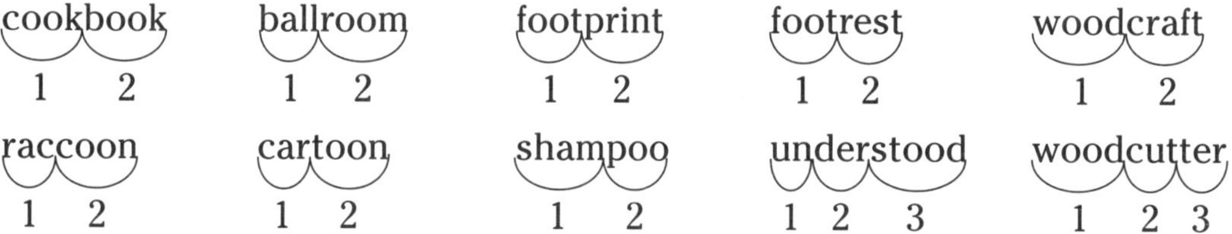

C. Word Parts. Say the word.

passive

D. Words with Word Parts. Say the words.

1. inlaw disgrace exceed preside
2. aggressive marvelous formal obtainable
3. amazement exclamation inactive concealment
4. exception contentment detachment preconception

E. Sight Words. Say the words.

learn	enough	among	minute	live
year	also	almost	sure	told

F. Passages. Read each part of the story. Write the story part number under the picture that goes with each story part.

Norm Learns More

Part 1

After dinner, Norm and Uncle Gregg returned to the den. Uncle Gregg placed some
14 wood in the fireplace and started a fire. "That feels good," Norm said as he stood by the
32 fire. "Will you tell me more about the cork farm now, Uncle Gregg?" he asked.
47 They sat down, and Norm's uncle began to talk. "Well, I told you that cork strippers
63 must be careful. If they cut too much cork or cut into the tree too deeply, they can hurt
82 the tree. Cork will never grow again in the spot where the tree has been hurt.
98 After the cork comes off the tree, the trunk of the tree turns a deep rust red. This is
117 because tannin, a kind of powder in the tree trunk, turns red when air hits it. Tannin
134 has many uses, but we can save that until your next report," Uncle Gregg said.

Part 2

149 Uncle Gregg also explained that Portugal sells most of its cork. "Since cork is so
164 important, there are rules to protect cork trees. One good rule is that a cork tree must be
182 fifteen to twenty years old before it is first stripped. A tree that has been stripped of cork
200 should not be stripped again until nine years have passed. Rules like these help keep the
216 trees in good shape. Trees that are well cared for live three hundred to four hundred years."
233 Uncle Gregg got up from his chair and went to stir the fire in the fireplace.

Part 3

249 "Cork is marvelous," Uncle Gregg said. "It is very light because it is ninety-two
263 percent air. It is not affected by heat, cold, liquids, or gas. It is also soundproof. Among
280 other things, cork is used to make bottle stoppers and place mats." Then Uncle Gregg
295 paused for a minute and said, "Well, Norm, I think I have told you all I know about cork.
314 Do you think you have learned enough to write a report?" he asked.
327 "I sure do, Uncle Gregg," Norm said. "Thank you for taking the time to explain all of
344 this to me. My report is sure to be the most unusual one in my class."
360

______ ______ ______

G. Practice Activity 1. Read each question. Look back at the story on page 129. Fill in each blank with the best word.

Part 1

1. How can cork strippers hurt a tree?

   They can cut too much ________________ or cut into the tree too ________________.

2. How does the tree trunk change after the cork comes off?

   The trunk turns a deep ________________ ________________.

3. What is the powder in the tree trunk called?

   The powder is called ________________.

Part 2

4. How old must a cork tree be before it is stripped?

   The cork tree must be ________________ to ________________ years old.

5. How many years must pass before a cork tree should be stripped again?

   At least ________________ years must pass before a cork tree can be stripped again.

6. How many years can a cork tree live?

   A cork tree that is well cared for can live ________________ ________________ to ________________ ________________ years.

Part 3

7. What percent of cork is air?

   ________________-________________ percent of cork is air.

8. What is cork used to make?

   Cork is used to make bottle ________________ and ________________ mats, among other things.

☐ Correct

H. **Practice Activity 2.** Read each story. Underline the endings that make sense.

1. Janis grows flowers in her garden. In the summer, Janis __________.
   a. shakes the snow off her plants
   b. looks at flowers blooming in the garden
   c. cuts the flowers off the plants

2. The winters in New York can be very cold. During one cold winter, Troy __________.
   a. put on a wool hood
   b. picked blooming flowers in the woods
   c. added wood to the fireplace

3. One afternoon, Gale went to the drugstore. At the drugstore, she got __________.
   a. a brook filled with water
   b. a book and a little wooden box
   c. a good book and a box of needles

4. One summer day, Maria went to the woods with her dog. In the woods, she __________.
   a. sat next to a brook
   b. stood on a footstool
   c. looked at the blooming flowers

☐ Correct

I. **Practice Activity 3.** Read each question. Underline the best words for each question.

1. Which words name animals?

footprint	giraffe
rabbit	raccoon
woodcraft	woodchuck

2. Which words name people?

woodcutter	bookkeeper
moonlight	footlocker
townspeople	cowhand

3. Which words name things you can get at a drugstore?

understood	toothbrush
toothpaste	shampoo
woodpile	footprint

4. Which words name things you can ride in or on?

seaplane	widower
rowboat	scooter
sailboat	stagecoach

5. Which words name rooms?

bedroom	fishhook
ballroom	woodcraft
kitchen	bathroom

6. Which words name tools?

blowtorch	hammer
screwdriver	footrest
wrench	crowbar

7. Which words name things you can find in a kitchen?

ballroom	teaspoon
scooter	faucet
cookbook	penthouse

8. Which words name sports?

football	sunflower
woodpile	baseball
soccer	nightgown

☐ Correct

LESSON 33

A. New Words. Say each sound. Say each word.

1. hook hoop
2. wool brook
3. bloom wood
4. took troops
5. My coat was caught on this hook.
6. The wool curtains will keep out the cold wind.
7. Put the wood by the fireplace, please.
8. The train trip to the seacoast took five days.

B. Challenge Words. Say the words.

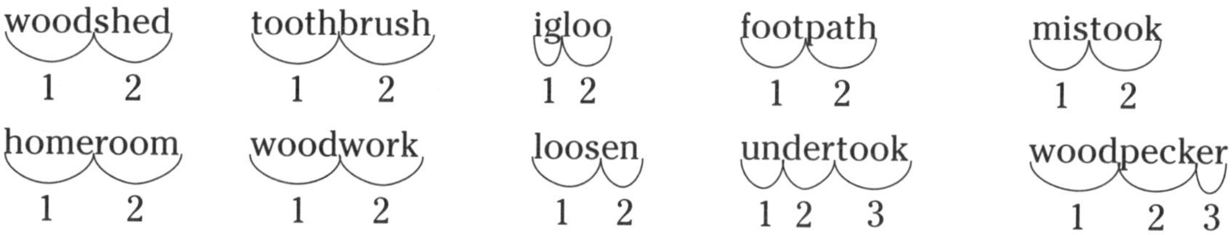

C. Word Parts. Say the word.

passive

D. Words with Word Parts. Say the words.

1. commute abuse refrain expel
2. offensive fatal flawless obsessive
3. discreetly constructive normally intersection
4. detachable resentment disrespectful exclusive

E. Sight Words. Say the words.

minute among enough learn only
their thought told your also

F. Passages. Read each part of the story. Write the story part number under the picture that goes with each story part.

Dad and the Scouts

Part 1

Dad drove the car into the driveway and said to Mike, "When you get out, don't
16 forget to take your sleeping bag and knapsack into the house. Tell Mom I will be there
33 in a few minutes." Mike took his things and went in while Dad put the car away. When
51 Dad went in, Mike was telling his mother all about their weekend camping trip.
65 Mom glanced at Dad, who looked exhausted. "Dinner will be in about an hour," she
80 said. "Why don't you rest a little? I can get all the details from Mike," she said, trying to
99 hide a smile.
102 "I think I could sleep for a week," Dad agreed as he sat down on the couch. "Call me if
122 you need any help."

Part 2

126 Later, at the dinner table, Mike continued to tell his mother about the things he and
142 the other boys in the scout troop had discovered in the woods. "We got to brush our
159 teeth in the brook, and we even saw a woodpecker," Mike told his mother. "We also
175 went for a long hike on the footpath around the lake. At night, we cooked hot dogs and
193 beans over a campfire. It was tremendous!" Mike exclaimed.
202 They finished eating, and Mike said, "All the scouts said to thank you, Dad. They said
218 you were a good sport too. I hope we can go back next year. Can we?"
234 "Let's wait and see, Mike," his dad said.

Part 3

242 After Mike was in bed, Mom said to Dad, "You look terrible! I thought you told Mike
259 you were an expert Eagle Scout when you were a boy. What happened to you?"
274 "Don't make me remember it all," Dad groaned. "To start with, no one told me the
290 tents had detachable flaps. I was the only scout leader who had to have a *kid* help him
308 put up his tent! The next day we went on a hike. I thought hikes were *short* trips. My
327 feet hurt so badly by the time we returned, I was ready to turn in all my Eagle Scout
346 badges. Then we discovered a fatal mistake. My tent must have been pitched right on
361 top of an anthill. The ant attack was in full swing by the time we got to my tent." Dad
381 looked at Mom who was grinning widely. "It's not that funny. Did I tell you about the
398 woodpecker that kept me awake all night with its pecking?"
408

______ ______ ______

G. Practice Activity 1. Read each question. Look back at the story on page 133. Fill in each blank with the best word.

Part 1

1. What did Dad and Mike do one weekend?

   They went on a ________________ ________________.

2. What did Mike take into the house?

   Mike took his ________________ bag and his ________________.

3. Who looked exhausted after the camping trip?

   ________________ looked exhausted after the camping trip.

Part 2

4. Where had the scouts hiked?

   The scouts had hiked on a footpath around the ________________.

5. What did the scouts do at night?

   At night, they cooked ________________ ________________ and ________________ over a campfire.

6. What did the scouts say about Mike's father?

   They said that his father was a good ________________.

Part 3

7. Why did Dad have ants in his tent?

   His tent was right on top of an ________________.

8. Why didn't Dad get any sleep on the camping trip?

   A ________________ kept Dad awake all night with his pecking.

☐ Correct

H. Practice Activity 2. Fill in each blank with the best word.

wool	**hook**	**brook**	**hood**
wood	**took**	**shook**	**good**

1. The baby ________________ her rattle.
2. Martha ________________ the children on a trip to the woods.
3. The ________________ of the car was hot after the drive.
4. Because of the cold wind, Gene put on a ________________ coat.
5. Would you rate this show as ________________ or bad?
6. The flowers grew along the little ________________.
7. Ted hung the plow blade on a large ________________.
8. The footstool was made of ________________.

☐ Correct

I. Practice Activity 3. Fill in each blank with the better word.

1. ________________ people who work at the same factory ________________ to work in one car. — commute, several
2. Because of Carla's ________________ acts in class, the principal had to ________________ Carla. — expel, terrible
3. The store got the ________________ ________________ of shirts just one day before the sale. — final, shipment
4. Every day Janis goes to an ________________ class. She feels ________________ after the class. — marvelous, exercise
5. Mark plans to continue his ________________ at a trade school for ________________. — adults, education
6. I was very ________________ when I heard the fire ________________ ring in the classroom. — alarm, afraid
7. This fall Kay plans to ________________ the number of ________________ in her herd to twenty. — cattle, increase

☐ Correct ☐ Checking Up

LESSON 34

■ **New Sound.** Say the words.

dread meant

A. New Words. Say each sound. Say each word.

1.	thread	death
2.	steal	meant
3.	spread	meal
4.	dream	scream

5. Please use green thread when you sew my socks.
6. I meant to say, "Turn right at the light."
7. Mick will spread the food out over the picnic table.
8. My dream job is to be a writer.

B. Challenge Words. Say the words.

weather (1 2)	peanut (1 2)	sunbeam (1 2)	headlight (1 2)	heavy (1 2)
homestead (1 2)	mealtime (1 2)	widespread (1 2)	seaweed (1 2)	leadership (1 2 3)

C. Words with Word Parts. Say the words.

1.	devise	compete	protest	confirm
2.	adjustable	dental	favorable	impressive
3.	extensive	amendment	defensive	convention
4.	collectively	innovation	meaningful	intermission

D. Sight Words. Say the words.

heard	minute	enough	learn	thought
friends	almost	does	anything	don't

E. Passages. Read each part of the story. Write the story part number under the picture that goes with each story part.

Death Scream

Part 1

Marty, Rick, Kate, and Pat were all sitting in the dining room at Pat's house. Three of
17 them were trying to convince Pat to come to the show with them. "You will have a good
35 time without me," she said. "*Death Scream* does not sound like anything I would enjoy.
50 Besides, the last time you dragged me to a show like that, I had bad dreams all night. I
69 am surprised you are going to see it, Kate," Pat said meaningfully.
81 "I told them that if it was too terrible to watch, I would get up and leave," Kate said. "I
101 heard that some parts of the film are impressive. I wish you would change your mind, Pat."
118 "Not a chance," Pat said, shaking her head.

Part 2

126 They continued discussing the film for a while. Finally, Kate, Rick, and Marty
139 decided that Pat was definitely not going with them. Since it was close to showtime,
154 they decided to leave. "I hope you all enjoy the show," Pat said sincerely as they left.
171 "Let me know how you like it," she said to Kate.
182 After her friends left, Pat spoke to her mother. Pat explained why she had chosen not to
199 go. "At one time, a film meant entertainment. I don't find it entertaining to be frightened out
216 of my wits. I prefer to stay home. I hope Kate does not regret going to see it."

Part 3

234 The next day, Pat saw Kate at school. "Well, how was it?" Pat asked.
248 "I hate to admit it, but it was dreadful. I was afraid the whole time. I think I screamed six
268 times. I was going to leave, but Rick and Marty teased me so much that I stayed. Besides, I
287 think I might have been more afraid to walk home alone than to stay there. I would not tell
306 the boys that, though. I sure learned my lesson! Next time I will stay home, too."
322 "I bet Rick and Marty were afraid, too," Pat said. "They will just refuse to admit it. I
340 wish there was a way we could find out what they really thought about it." Pat grinned.
357 "Let's ask around, shall we?"
362

F. Practice Activity 1. Read each question. Look back at the story on page 137. Fill in each blank with the best word.

Part 1

1. What did Marty, Rick, and Kate want Pat to do?

   They wanted Pat to come to the __________ with them.

2. What was the name of the show?

   The name of the show was __________ __________.

3. Why didn't Pat want to go to the show?

   She had bad __________ after the last time she went to a show like *Death Scream*.

Part 2

4. Who went to the show?

   __________, __________, and __________ went to the show.

5. Whom did Pat speak with when her friends left?

   Pat spoke with her __________.

Part 3

6. What did Kate say about the show?

   Kate said that the show was __________.

7. How did Kate feel during the show?

   She was __________ the whole time.

8. Why didn't Kate leave when she became afraid?

   Rick and Marty __________ her so much that she stayed.

☐ Correct

G. Practice Activity 2. Read each list. Cross out the word that does not belong in each list.

1.	lightning weather leadership thunder	4.	woodpecker giraffe gopher widespread	7.	homeroom headlight classmates classroom
2.	seaweed sagebrush pencil bamboo	5.	breakfast mealtime heavy dinner	8.	football basketball headlight soccer
3.	sunbeam moonlight seaweed flashlight	6.	peanut mushroom marshmallow homestead	9.	nightgown weather trousers jacket

☐ Correct

H. Practice Activity 2. Fill in each blank with the better word.

1. If you played a trumpet in a contest, you would ________________ in the contest. — complete / compete
2. If you went to a dentist, you would have some ________________ work done on your teeth. — dental / final
3. If you really liked something or were very impressed by something, it would be ________________. — impressive / negative
4. If you had a belt that could adjust to many sizes, the belt would be ________________. — adjustable / portable
5. If you really liked someone's plan and were in favor of it, the plan would be ________________ to you. — punishable / favorable
6. If you work out a plan to do something, you ________________ a plan. — devise / decrease
7. If you take a train to and from work every day, you ________________ by train. — commute / combine
8. If you had a number of plants in your greenhouse, you would have ________________ plants. — formal / several

☐ Correct

LESSON 35

A. New Words. Say each sound. Say each word.

1. heavy teach
2. wheat dread
3. heather cheap
4. beach dealt
5. I ate a heavy breakfast this morning.
6. What do you dread the most about airplane rides?
7. The purple heather grows on the hillside.
8. I dealt you some cards while you fixed our snacks.

B. Challenge Words. Say the words.

increase	leather	instead	meantime	pleasant
weapon	feather	cream puff	meadow	teacher

C. Words with Word Parts. Say the words.

1. index ablaze distress provoke
2. tentative dreadful pardonable effective
3. comprehensive reflective exhaustion expertness
4. commandment abrasive accomplish inventiveness

D. Sight Words. Say the words.

heard	though	minute	among	enough
friend	thought	another	any	over

E. **Passages.** Read each part of the story. Write the story part number under the picture that goes with each story part.

A Flawless Plan

Part 1

For several days after she saw *Death Scream*, Kate continued to talk to Pat about it.
16 "Did I tell you that the night I saw it, I had a difficult time falling asleep? The next
35 morning, my bedspread was all bunched up on the bed. I must have had bad dreams all
52 night. What a mistake that was! I wish I had stayed home instead. Have you heard
68 anything about what Rick and Marty thought of it?" Kate asked her friend.
81 "They claim it was a *mild* film and there was nothing to account for all your distress,"
98 Pat said. "I have another thought, though. Come over after school, and I will tell you
114 about it."

Part 2

116 After school, Pat and Kate sat on lawn chairs in the backyard, and Pat disclosed her
132 plan. "I have a feeling those boys were afraid, too. They are simply trying to provoke
148 you with all that talk about a 'mild' film. I think it's a cheap trick, so this is what we are
169 going to do. First, we need to make a deal with my little brother."
183 Kate looked puzzled. Pat said, "I heard the boys are having a meeting in their
198 clubhouse Thursday afternoon. All we need to do is to have Brad plant a tape recorder
214 inside the clubhouse. Then he will get Rick and Marty to talk about *Death Scream*. We
230 will get all their comments on tape."

Part 3

237 Thursday afternoon, Pat and Kate were waiting for Brad to put the tape recorder
251 inside the clubhouse. Kate asked Pat, "Did you have any problems with Brad? Does he
266 know what to do?"
270 "He knows what to do, the little crook! I have to clean his room for a week for this.
289 When Marty and Rick are in the clubhouse, Brad will bring them a bowl of popcorn.
305 Then Brad will ask them about the film and leave. I hope it works!"
319 Two hours later, the boys' meeting was over. Brad gave the tape recorder to his
334 sister and left with a pleasant smile. The girls checked different parts of the tape until
350 they heard Marty say, "We cannot let Kate or Pat find out. At one point, I thought I was
369 going to be sick. . . . I wanted Kate to leave so I could go, too. . . ." Pat and Kate grinned
387 when they heard this.
391

____

____

____

F. Practice Activity 1. Read each question. Look back at the story on page 141. Fill in each blank with the best word.

Part 1

1. What happened to Kate after she saw *Death Scream*?

   She had bad ________________ all night.

2. What did Kate wish she had done instead of going to the show?

   She wished that she had stayed ________________ instead of going to the show.

3. What did the boys say about the film?

   They said the film was very ________________.

Part 2

4. How did Pat think the boys felt about the show?

   Pat thought the boys were ________________, too.

5. What did Brad put inside the boys' clubhouse?

   He put a ________________ ________________ inside the boys' clubhouse.

6. What did the girls want the boys to talk about?

   They wanted the boys to talk about the film ________________

   ________________.

Part 3

7. What did the girls do with the tape recorder?

   They checked ________________ parts of the ________________.

8. What did the girls hear Marty say about the film?

   The girls heard Marty say that he thought he was going to be

   ________________ during the show.

☐ Correct

G. **Practice Activity 2.** Read each question. Underline the best words for each question.

1. Which words name people?
   teacher, widow
   cowhand, pleasant
   bookkeeper, homeowner
2. Which words name places?
   leather, bedspread
   meadow, feather
   homeroom, footpath
3. Which words name things?
   feather, teacher
   woodpecker, leather
   toothbrush, headlight
4. Which words name plants?
   sagebrush, woodpecker
   sunflowers, cabbage
   pine tree, cream puff
5. Which words tell about meals?
   mealtime, breakfast
   lunch, weapon
   picnic, dinner
6. Which words name things you can eat?
   peanut, marshmallow
   leather, toothbrush
   cream puff, chowder
7. Which words tell how you may feel?
   pleasant, woodshed
   unhappy, mealtime
   happy, terrific
8. Which words tell about weather?
   lightning, headlights
   outgrown, thunder
   sunshine, peanuts

☐ Correct

H. **Practice Activity 3.** Fill in each blank with the better word.

1. The ________________ of shells did not have a flaw. The collection was ________________. (flawless, collection)
2. Your lateness is ________________ if you have an ________________. (excuse, pardonable)
3. Seat belts need to be ________________. To operate ________________, seat belts need to be tight. (adjustable, safely)
4. A ________________ was placed on the lawn in front of the school. It is a monument to good ________________. (monument, education)
5. When Janis went to ________________ in the speech contest, she was ________________. (speechless, compete)
6. Every day Ms. Archer ________________ to work on an ________________ subway train. This subway train stops only twice. (commutes, express)

☐ Correct

LESSON 36

A. New Words. Say each sound. Say each word.

1. deaf heap
2. feast weather
3. health peach
4. bleach spread
5. Some fish in the deep sea are deaf.
6. Watch the weather report on the news.
7. My health club has a large swimming pool.
8. Sam likes to spread jam on his toast.

B. Challenge Words. Say the words.

pheasant (1 2)	seasick (1 2)	sweater (1 2)	preacher (1 2)	headdress (1 2)
seacoast (1 2)	spreader (1 2)	leaflet (1 2)	gingerbread (1 2 3)	letterhead (1 2 3)

C. Words with Word Parts. Say the words.

1. proceed alive precise excel
2. perceptive prosperous peaceable needless
3. progressive destructive prediction abolish
4. complaining preventive unskillfully astonishingly

D. Sight Words. Say the words.

though	enough	through	throughout	among
again	don't	year	thought	almost

E. Passages. Read each part of the story. Write the story part number under the picture that goes with each story part.

The Last Picnic

Part 1

Stan and Eve were in the kitchen packing the picnic basket. "I am glad the weather is
17 so nice," Eve said. "This is likely to be our last picnic this summer. The summer sure
34 went quickly, don't you think?"
39 "I agree," Stan said. "That's one reason I want to make this a real feast. So far I have
58 hot dogs and hamburgers, peaches, tea, and gingerbread cake. What other things do
71 we need?" asked Stan.
75 "We should take a blanket to sit on, and maybe we should take sweaters. The
90 seacoast gets cool at night. Barb and Jack will arrive soon. It's close to noon, and they
107 are both astonishingly precise."

Part 2

111 Shortly after noon, they packed the car and headed for Lighthouse Bay. "I hope you have
127 heaps of food in that basket," Jack said. "By the time we get there, I will be ready to eat."
147 "That's not news, Jack. I have known you to eat throughout the entire day," Eve said.
163 "It beats me how you stay so disgustingly thin."
172 "All that food keeps me in good health," Jack said with a grin. "My mother says I am
190 still a growing boy. Besides, don't forget that I run seven miles a day!" A short time
207 later they reached Lighthouse Bay and parked the car close to the beach.

Part 3

220 "Stan, spread the blanket by the rocks," called Barb. "I will set the food out, and we
237 can snack until the fire gets going."
244 "Eve and I will go find some bleached driftwood for the bonfire," Jack said. "Make
259 sure there is enough for us to eat when we get back. On second thought, maybe you
276 should get the driftwood, and we should spread out the food!"
287 They spent a pleasant afternoon playing ball, snacking, and swimming. Around six
299 they started the fire and roasted hot dogs and hamburgers. When it got dark, they
314 carefully doused the fire and got ready to leave. All agreed that the last picnic of the
331 summer had been the best one.
337

__________ __________ __________

F. Practice Activity 1. Read each question. Look back at the story on page 145. Fill in each blank with the best word.

Part 1

1. Why did Stan want to make the picnic a real feast?

   It was the ____________________ picnic of the summer.

2. What did Stan pack for the picnic?

   He packed hot ____________________, hamburgers, peaches, tea, and gingerbread ____________________.

3. Why did Eve think that they should take sweaters?

   She thought they should take sweaters because the seacoast gets ____________________ at ____________________.

Part 2

4. Where did they go for their picnic?

   They went to ____________________ ____________________.

5. What did Jack hope they had in the basket?

   He hoped that they had heaps of ____________________ in the basket.

6. Why does Jack stay so thin?

   One reason is that Jack runs ____________________ ____________________ a day.

Part 3

7. How did they spend the afternoon?

   They played ____________________, snacked, and went ____________________.

8. What did they all agree on at the end of the picnic?

   They all agreed that the last picnic of the summer had been the ____________________ one.

☐ Correct

G. **Practice Activity 2.** Read each story. Underline the endings that make sense.

1. One Saturday, Kay went to the store to get food for lunch. At the store, she got ________.
   a. a loaf of wheat bread
   b. cheese spread and crackers
   c. toothpaste and shampoo

2. Ms. Floyd likes to get things on sale. One day, Ms. Floyd got ________.
   a. two boxes of thread that were half-price
   b. a very thick steak for a high price
   c. six loaves of French bread for a very cheap price

3. Mark really likes to play checkers. On Thursday night, he ________.
   a. put the checkerboard on the table
   b. cooked steaks on a grill
   c. placed the checkers on the board

4. Barb takes very good care of her things. One morning, Barb ________.
   a. used a needle and thread to mend her bedspread
   b. placed her lace bedspread in a large box
   c. broke all of her heavy dishes

☐ Correct

H. **Practice Activity 3.** Fill in each blank with the better word.

1. If something has a heartbeat, it is ________________. — alive / abuse
2. If you are very good at a subject in school, you ________________ in that subject. — excel / excuse
3. If you had lots of wealth, you would be ________________. — numerous / prosperous
4. If you did something that did not need to be done, what you did was ________________. — needless / endless
5. If you went ahead and did something, you would ________________. — proceed / protest
6. If a house was on fire, the house would be ________________. — ablaze / alive
7. If a jewel did not have one flaw, it would be ________________. — nameless / flawless
8. If you have work done on your teeth, you would have ________________ work done. — normal / dental

☐ Correct ☐ Checking Up

Word Lists

LESSON 1

New Words
food
soon
feed
flirt
broom
flow
spoon
brain
smooth
choose
sport
tooth

Challenge Words
rooster
scooter
moonlight
cartoon
toothbrush
schoolroom
teaspoon
shampoo
raccoon
afternoon

Sight Words
all
call
hall
ball
tall
because
through
also
about
care
find
were
one
your
who
some
how
many

LESSON 2

New Words
moon
cool
show
noon
sheet
tool
shoot
moose
boast
boost
moan
snooze

Challenge Words
harpoon
moonbeam
whirlpool
noontime
monsoon
homeroom
classroom
plaintiff
harbor
increase

Sight Words
all
tall
ball
fall
call
because
also
through
about
find
where
your
now
how
why

LESSON 3

New Words
room
loose
stool
root
steal
roof
booth
mood
beach
hoop
lease
bloom

Challenge Words
dustproof
booster
loosen
baboon
tattoo
foolproof
mushroom
drainpipe
president
innkeeper

Sight Words
all
fall
call
hall
tall
about
because
want
through
also
put
now
one
find
been

LESSON 4

New Words
yawn
fault
claw
haul
float
draw
spool
crawl
cool
lawn
loan
cause

Challenge Words
exhaust
author
auburn
August
drawing
lawn mower
lawyer
igloo
imperfect
advertise

Sight Words
other
another
mother
brother
many
also
call
find
about
been
come
people
there
were

LESSON 5

New Words
fraud
straw
stool
dream
drawn
vault
hawk
freed
shawl
flow
flaw
flee

Challenge Words
applause
coleslaw
withdrawn
sawdust
drawback
autumn
sweepstakes
wayside
bridegroom
entertainment

Sight Words
other
another
brother
mother
many
also
animals
because
want
there
what
were
now
call

LESSON 6

New Words
law
choose
pause
lawn
thaw
sprawl
sprain
jaw
jar
paw
throw
launch

Challenge Words
pauper
sawmill
because
seesaw
awesome
launder
autoharp
automatic
misinterpret
understood

Sight Words
other
another
mother
brother
many
through
also
one
want
about
would
how
from
now

LESSON 7

New Words
boil
boy
point
paint
Roy
pawn
joy
soil
goose
coin
cool
noise

Challenge Words
turmoil
employ
enjoy
destroy
tinfoil
boycott
joyride
oyster
appointment
sharpshooter

Sight Words
old
cold
told
gold
sold
one
other
many
another
about
want
all
there
come
what

LESSON 8

New Words
join
jail
toy
tea
spoil
toil
maul
Floyd
spool
moist
crawl
Troy

Challenge Words
soybean
noiseless
annoy
loiter
exploit
toy shop
charcoal
corduroy
employee
employer

Sight Words
old
fold
cold
told
hold
give
other
about
through
find
all
would
were
there
want

LESSON 9	LESSON 10	LESSON 11	LESSON 12	LESSON 13	LESSON 14	LESSON 15
New Words	**New Words**	**New Words**	**New Words**	**New Words**	**New Words**	**New Words**
coil	new	chew	flew	out	our	sprout
coat	noise	paw	paws	joint	oil	coach
coy	grew	threw	blew	round	sound	couch
toy	grain	crew	new	shawl	cloud	sprawl
paints	chew	join	shrew	cloud	claw	trout
points	stew	blew	proof	loose	south	mouth
fail	news	grew	news	house	ground	haul
foil	fee	brew	stream	blew	mouse	grouch
pawn	dew	shown	drew	shout	scoot	spout
toil	drawn	joy	threw	proud	moist	ouch
tool	drew	crawl	strewn	blouse	scout	threw
poise	flew	shrew	joys	blown	hound	flour
Challenge Words	**Challenge Words**	**Challenge Words**	**Challenge Words**	**Challenge Words**	**Challenge Words**	**Challenge Words**
enjoy	jewel	sewer	newsstand	counter	without	outgrew
ointment	newsstand	cashew	Lewis	thousand	playground	dismount
poison	newscast	unscrew	sewer	surround	madhouse	farmhouse
convoy	chewable	mildew	dewdrop	countless	outside	account
broiler	New York	newborn	August	southwest	cloudless	countless
avoid	newspaper	newsreel	newsprint	doghouse	discount	Boy Scout
embroider	screwdriver	crewneck	frustrate	outburst	thundercloud	outlaw
disappoint	newsletter	seaplane	classmates	trousers	underground	scoutmaster
destroyer	subscribe	jeweler	proofread	outspoken	southwestern	outstanding
enjoyment	storekeeper	authorize	appointment	encounter	fellowship	counterclockwise
Sight Words	**Sight Words**	**Sight Words**	**Sight Words**	**Sight Words**	**Sight Words**	**Sight Words**
old	find	find	find	walk	walk	walk
cold	mind	mind	mind	talk	talk	talk
sold	kind	kind	kind	coming	warm	woman
fold	over	give	over	woman	woman	women
told	give	over	give	even	even	over
give	told	mother	told	now	over	even
many	about	one	other	kind	kind	warm
other	another	told	another	want	also	there
also	what	your	through	about	through	told
through	who	about	want	another	went	come
come	could	where	all	cold	mother	many
were	come	many	about	some	give	where
there	now	why	many			
work	good					
find						

LESSON 16	LESSON 17	LESSON 18	LESSON 19	LESSON 20	LESSON 21	LESSON 22	LESSON 23
New Words	**New Words**	**New Words**	**New Words**	**New Words**	**New Words**	**New Words**	**New Words**
knot	phone	know	dodge	ridge	hitch	cell	force
wreck	quest	phone	catch	pitch	bridge	glance	mice
quit	phase	wrench	edge	phone	switch	stick	cause
knight	quiz	quit	sketch	know	math	cone	cinch
phone	math	knife	judge	grudge	nudge	voice	place
knob	wring	wrung	snatch	quote	Mitch	twice	crow
graph	phrase	wrist	witch	fudge	ditch	clip	since
knife	quake	thick	chase	hatch	blotch	space	cape
wrote	quote	quick	patch	badge	budge	trick	fence
kneel	quite	knew	itch	match	scratch	peace	cease
quilt	write	sphinx	lodge	wedge	swish	came	crawl
wrap	knit	knelt	lock	path	latch	cent	price
Challenge Words	**Challenge Words**	**Challenge Words**	**Challenge Words**	**Challenge Words**	**Challenge Words**	**Challenge Words**	**Challenge Words**
dolphin	gopher	sulphur	catcher	hatchback	pitchfork	circus	cartwheel
wrapper	knapsack	playwright	hodgepodge	pitchfork	drawbridge	canteen	center
jackknife	quiver	unknown	pitcher	misjudge	stretcher	blockade	embrace
shipwreck	orphan	liquid	outstretch	phonics	hopscotch	cinder	cedar
knapsack	shipwreck	knuckle	hatchet	bamboo	switchover	absence	pencil
knothole	knockout	phantom	hitchhike	coastline	graphite	spacecraft	kneecap
vanquish	banquet	writer	patchwork	authentic	gopher	second	democrat
kneecap	wrinkle	tranquil	kitchen	autograph	yard line	electric	committee
underline	emphasis	squirrel	underneath				
handwritten	equipment	sophomore	referee				
Sight Words	**Sight Words**	**Sight Words**	**Sight Words**	**Sight Words**	**Sight Words**	**Sight Words**	**Sight Words**
don't	sure	sure	only	even	their	every	heard
even	don't	only	most	does	only	their	any
coming	care	again	does	most	most	does	every
find	even	hold	again	only	even	only	their
two	two	about	sure	again	does	sure	don't
sure	were	your	four	through	many	told	talk
work	should	also	also	their	also	find	about
about	about	give	many	many	find	your	some
told	put	want	some	also	some	talk	through
woman	others	would	walk	about	over	again	there
give			another				
machine			hour				

LESSON 24	LESSON 25	LESSON 26	LESSON 27	LESSON 28	LESSON 29	LESSON 30	LESSON 31
New Words	**New Words**	**New Words**	**New Words**	**New Words**	**New Words**	**New Words**	**New Words**
prance	cringe	germ	surge	owl	frown	flower	book
curb	cage	stage	goose	blown	brow	crow	shook
couch	gee	gem	gist	flown	growl	crown	bloom
cliff	gent	age	green	plow	slow	town	cook
cents	glee	glad	pages	clown	growth	grow	stood
prince	merge	urge	gash	show	bowl	powder	spool
choice	gust	large	bulge	down	shown	gown	fool
crew	page	goose	glee	crowd	brown	glow	foot
lace	strange	grew	range				
cool	change	drug	stage				
nice	gate	Gene	merge				
Rick	gist	sponge	ranger				
Challenge Words	**Challenge Words**	**Challenge Words**	**Challenge Words**	**Challenge Words**	**Challenge Words**	**Challenge Words**	**Challenge Words**
citrus	margin	ginger	drugstore	showtime	snowdrift	cowhide	woodpile
faucet	gently	disgust	danger	grown-up	downstream	rowboat	football
playwright	cabbage	target	gateway	owner	snowplow	nightgown	scooter
census	percent	sagebrush	carpool	chowder	homeowner	penthouse	wooden
boycott	teenage	greenhouse	giraffe	cowhand	blowtorch	outgrown	teaspoon
cloister	sausage	stagecoach	urgent	crowbar	fellowship	sunflower	moonlight
civil	German	Pacific	congress	sundown	gunpowder	widower	fishhook
countess	grapevine	gingersnap	autograph	somehow	townsman	marshmallow	mushroom
							bookkeeper
							footlocker
Sight Words	**Sight Words**	**Sight Words**	**Sight Words**	**Sight Words**	**Sight Words**	**Sight Words**	**Sight Words**
any	father	father	year	thought	thought	friend	enough
every	year	year	father	friend	someone	thought	learn
their	their	care	don’t	anyway	friend	almost	anything
don’t	every	women	give	someone	only	anyone	thought
only	again	any	does	somehow	any	every	almost
one	even	their	many	were	their	over	only
kind	two	talk	hold	sure	care	sure	don’t
another	many	over	through	two	over	told	father
from	others	other	also	their	sure	another	sure
walk	through	also	mind	kind	don’t	even	does

LESSON 32	LESSON 33	LESSON 34	LESSON 35	LESSON 36
New Words	**New Words**	**New Words**	**New Words**	**New Words**
hood	hook	thread	heavy	deaf
spool	hoop	death	teach	heap
hook	wool	steal	wheat	feast
crook	brook	meant	dread	weather
gloom	bloom	spread	heather	health
good	wood	meal	cheap	peach
brook	took	dream	beach	bleach
boost	troops	scream	dealt	spread
Challenge Words	**Challenge Words**	**Challenge Words**	**Challenge Words**	**Challenge Words**
cookbook	woodshed	weather	increase	pheasant
ballroom	toothbrush	peanut	leather	seasick
footprint	igloo	sunbeam	instead	sweater
footrest	footpath	headlight	meantime	preacher
woodcraft	mistook	heavy	pleasant	headdress
raccoon	homeroom	homestead	weapon	seacoast
cartoon	woodwork	mealtime	feather	spreader
shampoo	loosen	widespread	cream puff	leaflet
understood	undertook	seaweed	meadow	gingerbread
woodcutter	woodpecker	leadership	teacher	letterhead
Sight Words	**Sight Words**	**Sight Words**	**Sight Words**	**Sight Words**
learn	minute	heard	heard	though
enough	among	minute	though	enough
among	enough	enough	minute	through
minute	learn	learn	among	throughout
live	only	thought	enough	among
year	their	friends	friend	again
also	thought	almost	thought	don't
almost	told	does	another	year
sure	your	anything	any	thought
told	also	don't	over	almost